THE MODERN MIND

Peer Reviews of *The Modern Mind*

Dr. Wall has written an important book giving an overview of the development of philosophy in the West from the Enlightenment to the end of the Second World War. His early death delayed its publication. There were many currents that formed the modern mind and Wall has a canny insight and the skill to lead his readers from the dawn of the Enlightenment in the early 1600's to the origins of Linguistic Analysis schools on the eve of WWI. Even if the quarrels of the eighteenth and nineteenth century have largely been forgotten, Dr. Wall's book is still timely because the modern mind was formed through those discussions and they are very much alive forming the minds of our contemporaries. I should warn the reader that while the style of this book is written as if for beginners (and they will profit from it) it does demand an understanding of the development of the major European currents of philosophy during those 250 years.

    Hilary Martin O.P. Fr. Martin has revealed the *primitive* mind's grasp of reality in his books *The Reality of Myth* and *People from the Dawn*.

In this book, Fr. Kevin Wall presents a brief, masterful overview of the vast sweep of modern and contemporary philosophy, tracing "the emergence of the modern mind" with all its doubts, hopes, promises, and perplexities. He makes special note of challenges and opportunities this presents for Thomism, as now "it must necessarily overflow its boundaries and seek to penetrate into others. It cannot be indifferent to other thought but must seek to illuminate and understand it. Not by pride in the possession of truth, but by such love for it, Thomism must bring its light to bear upon the many obscurities of the modern mind" (p. 112).

Michael J. Dodds, O.P., Professor of Philosophy and Theology, Dominican School of Philosophy and Theology, Berkeley, CA. Professor Dodds has published extensively on the interactions of science and religion.

In his searching study, *The Modern Mind*, Kevin Wall, O.P., gives us an historically grounded diagnosis of the malaise of modernity and post-modernity. Wall's range is impressive: Plato and Aristotle, Hegel and Kant, the dialectics of the Idealists and the varieties of existentialism. His account closes with the rise and fall of positivism. The dynamic heart of Wall's vision is the wisdom of the perennial philosophy, always alive in its engagement with the human struggle for truth. *The Modern Mind* serves us well as a serious introduction to the increasingly "interesting times" in which we now find ourselves.

James G. Hanink, Ph.D. President, American Maritain Association. Dr. Hanink, formerly a professor of philosophy at Loyola Marymount University, as an independent scholar writes in the areas of metaphysics, epistemology, and social thought.

Kevin Wall's book *The Modern Mind* offers a brief yet balanced account of the development of modern philosophical thought from the scientific revolution to the mid-twentieth century. As it proceeds, it offers a sustained critique from the perspective of modernity itself, largely by way of the thought of Kierkegaard, as well as representatives of earlier epochs, particularly Aristotle and Aquinas. By its brevity it offers a helpful introduction that may be supplemented by further study.

Fr. Brian Chrzastek, O.P., Assistant Professor of philosophy at the PFIC of the Dominican House of Studies, Washington D.C.

THE MODERN MIND:

EVOLUTION OF THE WESTERN WORLDVIEW

by

Kevin Wall

Editor: Dominic Colvert

Solas Press
Palo Alto
2020

Copyright © 2020 Solas Press. All rights reserved. No part of this book may be reproduced, stored in a retrieval system, or transmitted in any form, or by any means without the prior written permission of the publisher, except by a reviewer, who may quote brief passages in a review. PERMISSIONS: SOLAS PRESS, PO Box 60628, Palo Alto, CA. 94306 USA. www.solaspress.com.

Library of Congress Cataloging-in-Publication Data

Names: Wall, Kevin Albert, 1921-1988, author. | Colvert, Dominic, 1932- editor.

Title: The modern mind : evolution of the western worldview / Kevin Wall ; editor, Dominic Colvert.

Description: Palo Alto : Solas Press, 2020. | Includes bibliographical references and index. | Summary: "In the twenty-first century the wonders of science show its magnificent potential for good. The scientific successes we enjoy are rooted in the modern way of thinking about physics. But success has fostered a myth that the dialectic of physics should be used in other areas. In the opening paragraph the author proclaims-and indeed others agree-a crisis has been reached in our evolving Western worldview. In this work Kevin Wall illuminates this development in the light of philosophy, theology, science, art, and with reference to Greek and Scholastic minds--showing the real-world implications of Western speculative thought"-- Provided by publisher.

Identifiers: LCCN 2020018076 (print) | LCCN 2020018077 (ebook) | ISBN 9781893426092 (print edition) | ISBN 9781893426108 (ebook)

Subjects: LCSH: Philosophy--History.

Classification: LCC B72 .W325 2020 (print) | LCC B72 (ebook) | DDC 190--dc23

LC record available at https://lccn.loc.gov/2020018076

LC ebook record available at https://lccn.loc.gov/202001807

TABLE OF CONTENTS

Foreword — v
Editor's Note — xi

PART I THE ENLIGHTENMENT

CHAPTER 1
THE TENSION OF THE MODERN MIND — 1

CHAPTER 2
THE EMERGENCE OF THE MODERN MIND THROUGH SCIENCE — 5

CHAPTER 3
POSITIVISM: THE PRIME PHILOSOPHY OF THE MODERN MIND — 9

CHAPTER 4
HUME'S ATTACK UPON THE SUPPOSITIONS OF SCIENTIFIC METHODOLOGY AND KANT'S APOLOGETIC CRITIQUE — 15

CHAPTER 5
HEGELIAN CORRECTIVES — 21

CHAPTER 6
REFLECTIONS AND ASSESSMENT — 29

CHAPTER 7
FURTHER REFLECTIONS AND ASSESSMENT — 39

CHAPTER 8
**THE DYNAMISM OF THOUGHT
AS THE ULTIMATE SENSE OF KANT AND HEGEL**   43

CHAPTER 9
**THE DYNAMISM OF WILL:
SIN IN EXISTENTIAL THOUGHT**   53

CHAPTER 10
THE ROOTS OF THE KIERKEGAARDIAN REACTION   57

CHAPTER 11
KIERKEGAARD'S SPECULATIVE THOUGHT   63

CHAPTER 12
KIERKEGAARD'S ETHICS AND AESTHETICS   67

CHAPTER 13
THE KIERKEGAARDIAN MEANING OF LIFE   77

CHAPTER 14
VARIETIES OF EXISTENTIAL DOCTRINE   89

CHAPTER 15
AN EVALUATION OF EXISTENTIAL DOCTRINE   103

PART II ANALYTIC PHILOSOPHY

CHAPTER 16
LOGICAL ATOMISM   115

CHAPTER 17
IDEAL LANGUAGE   121
                    CHAPTER 18
LOGICAL POSITIVISM   129
                    CHAPTER 19
POST-WAR DEVELOPMENTS   141

INDEX   153

FOREWORD

OUR PLACE IN THE HISTORY OF PHILOSOPHY

What is and to what end do we study the history of philosophy? Is it to gain mere empirical knowledge of various theories proposed over time? Then it may be an exercise of philology rather than philosophy—and we would not learn what we ourselves should think. But we may learn something if, for example, there is something paradigmatic about certain positions in history. Then the identification of certain "types" (in the sense of Max Weber or Karl Jaspers) will help us to develop a "sapiential" approach to philosophy. It may still not teach us directly what to think. In fact, it will rather allow us to step away from the development of our own arguments and proposals and come to understand the place of our own thought in a range of possible positions that we may need to balance. It thus prevents us from becoming myopic in our own philosophical labors.

If we take this history not only as a history of perennial types but as a linear development of which we are currently the end point, then the history of philosophy will also be helpful in suggesting *critical* perspectives for our own day. We may come to understand better who we are and what we think, because we understand our reflections to be the result of earlier conversations (an idea that started with Johann von Herder's "genetic method"). This may perhaps be like a sort of collective psychoanalysis, though ideally it would consist of a genesis of philosophical reasoning and not so much of psychological causalities.

The history of philosophy may also allow us to evaluate critically certain positions from the perspective of their historical consequences. Thus, the program of modern science and philosophy as developed by Descartes and Bacon was meant to serve our self-preservation by making us "masters and possessors" of nature again, undoing the fall of Adam and Eve and our human condition not by divinely offered salvation but by technology. Seen across history, we now know that this program failed on its own terms, dialectically: it is the same technology that was to overcome famine, illness and death; which now threatens to destroy the planet environmentally, by atomic warfare, or by artificial intelligence taking over our life. The "subordination of life under the conditions of its preservation" (Theodor Adorno) leads to its own destruction; the disregard for the formal and final causes of life for the sake of material and efficient causes destroys life itself and leaves us without orientation. The study of the history of philosophy makes visible what we should not do, or forget, or discard.

The study of the history of philosophy also raises the question, whether history itself, philosophical or otherwise, has its own peculiar intelligibility, i.e., whether there is a narrative that can itself be understood in terms of philosophical concepts. In other words: is there only a history of philosophy, or also a philosophy of history?

From my reading of Kevin Wall's book *The Modern Mind*, it somehow addresses *all* of these questions in its survey of various schools of modern and contemporary thought: it is typological and critical, and it attempts to find an intelligible trajectory for the development of these schools—all with an eye towards understanding our current predicament.

Thomas Aquinas almost never addresses questions of this kind (perhaps with the exception of occasionally echoing Aristotle's narrative on the development of the pre-Socratics). Nor have Thomists done much more (with the exception of perhaps Jacques Maritain, though he sees the philosophy of history as a species of practical philosophy—something akin to the old *historia magistra vitae*). Can there be a Thomist philosophy of history?

While Thomists may be more modest than Hegel in their hope of finding intelligibility in empirical history, they may agree with him that the history of *philosophy* may be our most promising starting point. After all, philosophy embodies its own age in the form of thought; it is the most explicit form of the *Zeitgeist* and closely related to its religion and art. Philosophy's spirit explains in its own way why history occurs, for philosophy is inherently restless. It continues to reflect on earlier thought, never remaining the same but, as philosophy, unfolding with a certain kind of logic that allows for a coherent narrative. In this process, forms of thought are neither mere opinions, nor simply true or false, but—for Hegel—necessary stages on the way to a telos. Current philosophy as a response to the previous history of thought includes what went before and is therefore not complete without an understanding of this history itself. That this history is a *long* one illustrates for Hegel the greatness of the task, with its richness in perennial forms of thought and the necessary labor of concepts that it takes to develop them. (see Georg Wilhelm Friedrich Hegel, *History of Philosophy*, vol. III (Frankfurt am Main: Suhrkamp 2013), 506-509.)

If this history is to be intelligible, it must have a structuring principle, i.e., some kind of teleology or final causality. For nothing moves, unless it is for an end, and for the actualization of a potency. This may leave open the question of whether the default development is from act to potency—as it is in Heidegger: *Verfallenheit* or *Ruinanz* as a form of entropy, a view made most plausible from the phenomena of decadence in individual cultures. Or whether it is from potency to act, as in Hegel, perhaps more plausible given the overall development of humanity but leaving open the question of the actualizing efficient cause. Other suggestions may be more cyclical in kind (as in Oswald Spengler) or without any trajectory (as in Hans-Georg Gadamer).

But what is the actualization in question? What is its telos? Since it is the history of humanity, it must have a human telos, namely the flourishing of the human person as a social and rational animal. As such, humanity's forms of life are biologically underdetermined and therefore unfold not in the cycles of nature, but in a historical sequence across generations. For Kevin Wall, this telos is human self-understanding or "self-possession," though ultimately culminating in metaphysics and knowledge of God; for, "only he who knows God, knows man," as St. John Paul II. liked to quote Romano Guardini.

In this development, the history of *philosophy* will trace the most essential faculties of humanity—our spiritual faculties. Spiritual though they are, there are nevertheless interesting analogies to be made with our lower faculties. *Procreation*, for example, can serve as an analogue for what it means to "conceive" a thought (even in the triune God, it is understood as the *filiation* of a logos). Procreation also parallels our spiritual history's transgenerational telos, as it serves the survival of the species, and may thereby offer itself as a model for the history of thought.

Nutrition, by contrast, serves the survival of the *individual*. However, nutrition too can be taken as an analogue for the life of the mind, as we "digest" the world in our thoughts. Reality is "food for thought." Hegel (the subject of Wall's doctoral thesis) somewhere compares the mind to a ruminant, perhaps reflectively regurgitating its history of thought. While this kind of metabolism seems forward-looking and creative, Wall more drastically looks at the reverse act of *vomiting* as an analogue for the mental life. Vomiting, though negative, also reveals the teleology: it is the reaction to a reality that is indigestible, something not fit for the telos of the human mind. Mind is teleological: it is meant for knowledge and that means for truth (that is why we cannot "know" a falsehood). Something contrary to truth is hurled out, it is leaping out of the mouth. It is not object, but "abject" (as some may say today). If the history of thought proceeds by such leaps, by hurling out, then it is more akin to Kierkegaard's leaps from stage to stage than Hegel's logical progression of thought; it proceeds not by conclusion, but by revulsion. Like Kierkegaard, it also appeals to the will and characterizes that which revolts us as "sin." False forms of philosophy are part of a "sinful speculative life," stopping short on the way to ultimate intelligibility and self-knowledge that ever eludes us on this path, leading to darkness and disintegration of the self.

These shortcomings can be characterized by two "types," and they correspond to the Thomist understanding of the division of *being* into act and potency. The most fundamental forms of act and potency are *esse* and *essentia* and consequently "essentialist" and "existentialist" forms of thought can constitute the most fundamental dichotomy in the history of philosophy. A completed telos, one that is not triggering nausea and vomiting, must combine these two within the unified (and in this sense "simple") science of being, metaphysics. It is only from this unified perspective and from the awareness of its history that our current situation becomes visible as a form of schizophrenia: On the one hand, we believe that natural science offers us the ultimate intelligibility of all reality in its unalterable forms (laws of nature). On the other hand, we believe that there is no understanding of reality that is not alterable and indeed arbitrarily shaped by cultures, the powers of society or individual projects. Current science claims to show that we do not have free will, while postmodern thought tells us that everything is and must be our choice.

Science gives us the *facts* but leaves no place for *values* or choices (arbitrary or not). Essentialist thought seems more at ease with science (though the reasons for that await further explanation), whereas existentialist thinkers are revolted by the gap left by essentialists and scientists. They are thinkers of freedom and often of nihilism, if negation is the only response left in the face of the facts.

But there are other dichotomies as well: essentialists seek ideal languages; existentialists gravitate towards ordinary language, if not indirect communication. Essentialists tend to be metaphysical pluralists, like Bertrand Russell, whereas the existentialists at least aim at an ultimate, unified whole of life as the source of meaning. Essentialists want to eliminate existence predication (or reduce it to silence, as in the Wittgensteins' *Tractatus*), while existentialists ask about the meaning of that which has thus been eliminated: being.

In the telling of Kevin Wall, this unfolds in a historical development, where material science, which is a mere means for self-possession, is taken as the ultimate end, thus making self-understanding impossible—for a self cannot be material. This initially triggers the "vomiting" of David Hume, who challenges the claims of science to universal laws of causality in the face of the empirical, contingent, and always limited sense data. Kant in response tries to contain the vomit with the a priori forms of the mind, but to the exclusion of God. The German Idealists in turn try to reintegrate and re-digest the vomit by considering it to be a product of the mind as well (which thus is a ruminant); as a result, they must also claim to be God. Kierkegaard finally shows that this will not work, and that science cannot become the creator of its own subject matter. His leap out of this scheme towards true self-knowledge consists in knowing oneself to be a dependent creature in relationship with God, who freely created us and whom we choose to obey in faith.

Wall's sympathies appear to be with such existentialism, seeing its nausea as a possible gateway for Thomists into modern forms of thought. But he also acknowledges the possible emptiness of its response, which with a certain arbitrariness allows existentialists to be atheists like Heidegger and Sartre, but also agnostics like Karl Jaspers, and theists like Kierkegaard and Gabriel Marcel. As an ultimate answer, we may conclude, existentialism should also leave us disgusted, without motivation, and in despair.

Since the history of philosophy is intelligible only under a telos, does it also tell how it will end? Will it continue as a meaningless back and forth between essentialism and existentialism, rationalism and voluntarism, realism and nominalism, Utopia and Machiavelli, rationalism and empiricism, idealism and existentialism, science and fideism? Or will the revulsions and reactions provoke each other to ever greater extremes, such that they will end, not in a Hegelian sublation, but in disaster and in an apocalyptic eschaton? Or will it all simply peter out in entropy? Claiming that we know the answer to these questions may mean that we have yet again missed the telos of this history: or have not come to a proper grasp of ourselves as long as we do not know that we are not God, who alone is the Lord of history.

Anselm Ramelow, O.P.

Dominican School of Philosophy and Theology, Berkeley, CA

EDITOR'S NOTE

Kevin Wall died unexpectedly in 1988. He was a revered teacher who could illuminate philosophical ideas for the critical minds of his students from his encyclopedic reach into philosophy, science, theology, and art. Much of his estate was organized in notebooks, three-ring binders, and computer floppy disks. I became the custodian of this collection.

In the collection, his incomplete manuscript on the modern mind with its clearly prophetic observations was of great interest. It was evident that he had labored for several years on Western thinking and the dialectical science that has dominated it. He says, "The prime speculative error of the modern mind was to regard dialectical science as potential to nothing higher."

In the present work I bring together his critique of the underlying concepts of later Continental and English philosophy that underlie much of our day-to-day thinking. In doing this I am grateful for the consultations with Fr. Antoninus Wall, O.P. and Fr. James Thompson, O.P.

I have taken it to be an editor's best strategy to present his notes without alterations, except, of course, for obvious typos and grammatical slips. This work contains unusually perceptive and incisive ideas, although there were places too where the notes hint that maybe the written note did not represent his final thinking. Under the circumstances this volume lacks the overarching plan the author would have given it; however, it makes very clear many profound insights into transcendental elements of the modern mind and the attendant dangers.

Dominic Colvert

Part I

The Enlightenment

CHAPTER 1

THE TENSION OF THE MODERN MIND

The tension of the modern and contemporary mind differs from that of the past quantitatively not qualitatively. The rise and fall of this or that particular society alone is no longer the concern. Now the concern is for the fall of humankind as a whole.

The advance of science, good as it is in itself, has made this possible. This has led some to think that things in themselves, i.e., independently of human reason and will, have no intelligibility and no value. Chance, not thought or choice, is the radical cause. And the appearance of intelligible pattern or teleology is simply that—appearance. The underlying reality is the random collision of blind atoms.

Undoubtedly this notion has scientific value, but it has no acceptable social or artistic value. No one who seeks after social justice thinks that it is a purely subjective fiction with no relation to reality. No Jew could believe that those who suffered the holocaust will not be vindicated.

In the light of classical thought, the modern and contemporary search for unity is thoroughly understandable, whether the unity sought is essential or existential. Positivism seeks essential unity, and this makes existence intelligible—being is rational being.

Existentialism, on the other hand, seeks the unity of existence which it more or less identifies with volition, choice, and the irrational—Being is the being of choice. By choosing, man makes his essence. By his choice, he makes values and truth. And values and truth—the myth and the ontology—have their existence in the choice. They are that which stands over and against the choice as the posited and the positing. They are "essence" over and against "existence." To exist is to choose. And the very word can then be warped, as it were, to conform to this interpretation. To choose is to posit one's "essence" (read "nature"), and this is, as it were, to project oneself into the object of the choice or, passively, to go outside of oneself and, as going outside, to be outside, that is to say, *ex-existere*. From this point of view, there can be no tension except one which choice itself creates. No nature forces it to create an essence that does violence to its freedom. It itself creates whatever tensions exist. From the formal point of view, this interprets human choice as tradition interpreted the divine. It is a solipsistic atheism.

This should make it questionable to the critical contemporary person, that either reason or will can provide a solution. Reason's attempt to find one, which runs from Locke through Hume and Kant to Hegel was a failure. So was the attempt of will in Schopenhauer and Nietzsche and the many modern Existentialisms. Thus, both have accentuated the conflict rather than suppressing it. Linguistic Philosophy has been a late effort to break out through language. But this too has only shown that, when the ground of language is fully explicated, it shows the same conflict between "ought" and "is," between "myth" and "history." The critical analogical study of language does not overcome the conflict, but simply reveals it again.

Up to now, this analysis has been made by a philosophical reflection upon thought and will. It could just as well be made by a non-philosophical explication of non-reflective thought and volition: that of the majority of human beings. Those who experience the conflict only on this non-reflective level may hope that a more profound reflective understanding will overcome it. But the philosopher, who actually reflects, knows better. This is the common denominator of contemporary philosophical experience. Yet, both inescapably want to overcome the conflict and seek to do so by social action. Political and economic ideologies become their desperate way out.

The contemporary mind, therefore, partly feels that no one can find the answer and partly that economic or political ideologies can. Hence the attraction of Marxists, but also their repulsion. For the contemporary mind, Hegel claims to know too much, but, under the form of Marxism, perhaps to have the answer.

Nihilism, on the contrary, knows nothing, believes nothing and seeks nothing. Nihilists are Nietzsche's post-Christians whose experience of Christian culture has convinced them that there is no truth and no value. Nietzsche saw this conviction not as a loss but a gain through which modern European man could discard a debilitating Christianity and jettison his crippling obeisance to mediocre mass will. The excellent will of the superior man would then emerge, and his morality would either gain the ascendancy or, at the very least, seriously influence the course of history. Transvaluation rather than devaluation would then occur.

To most contemporary men, Nietzsche's expectations for will seem just as excessive as Hegel's claims for thought. Medieval man could agree with this assessment but would then see the situation in a different light. In Hegel's *Geist*, he would see a resurrected Neo-Platonism.[1] In Nietzsche's Superman, he would see Aquinas' Christ.[2] Contemporary taste finds both of these improbable and unpalatable, but, at the same time, strangely fascinating. Hegel and Nietzsche stir deep currents in the contemporary psyche.

In the present cultural milieu, what remains of traditional values are being further jettisoned. We will soon have lost most of them and will then confront the brutal facts of human existence unarmed. We will then learn what these abandoned values really did for us. And we will be forced to resurrect them, if this is possible, and again give meaning to our lives.

We must therefore recollect our past now, and by this recollection, assimilate it and thereby develop true historical consciousness. This may help us to understand what has caused our present fear that human existence has no sense at all. Through the emergence of the modern mind this has arisen. For a proper self-understanding it is, therefore, crucial that we discover how this occurred.

---

[1] Georg W. F. Hegel, *The Phenomenology of Spirit*.

[2] F. Nietzsche, *Thus Spoke Zarathustra*.

CHAPTER 2

THE EMERGENCE OF THE MODERN MIND THROUGH SCIENCE

The modern mind, in its scientific component, first emerged when empirical science began to develop in the post Renaissance period. It was chiefly an advance in the quantitative study of terrestrial and celestial phenomena. Induction began more adequately to match the quantitative facts of mechanical motion.

By measuring the positions of celestial bodies with greater precision than ever before, Tycho Brahe (1546-1601) revealed that they diverged sensibly from those which Ptolemaic theory predicted. Johannes Kepler (1571-1630) discovered from this that the planets followed elliptical rather than circular paths. He was then able to discover new quantitative relations between the geometrical components of the ellipses and the movement of the celestial bodies in time. These required a new formulation of the laws of celestial mechanics. Galileo Galilei (1564-1642) discovered new mathematical relations for the movements of bodies near the surface of the earth. These required a new formulation of the laws of terrestrial mechanics. Isaac Newton (1643-1727), then, in his generalized laws of motion, combined Kepler's and Galileo's results into one unified quantitative theory.

This new theory, using the mathematical tools of analytical geometry and the calculus, provided a method of analysis for mechanical motion whose possibilities seemed limitless. Impressed by this, the followers of Newton reevaluated its significance. It was no longer, as Newton had thought of it and as he had entitled his epoch-making book, *The Mathematical Principles of Natural Philosophy*, but a *substitute* for the natural philosophy of the medieval scholastics.

Galileo, Kepler and Newton had used induction to achieve their results in the logical arguments for passing from particular cases to universals. The results were so impressive that they commanded common assent. The laws of Newtonian dynamics seemed surely universal and necessary. Newtonian dynamics was a true science!

David Hume (1711-1776) attacked this evaluation, he denied Newtonian inductions were universal and necessary. He proposed that no induction could be of that character, that their supposed universality is a subjective anticipation. The true statement of the value of Newton's laws would be rather of the form: "on the basis of a finite number of observations, I anticipate that all bodies in the universe will attract each other in the inverse square of their distances apart..." The qualification which precedes the supposedly universal law expresses subjective anticipation only and imposes no necessity on objective nature.

Hume argued that this must be so since the induction is finite and cannot therefore conclude to the infinite. From "many" one could not argue to "all". The universally respected Newtonian dynamics was therefore vitiated by the subjective. Hume's argument was, at best, an expression of a strong anticipation that universal and necessary science is impossible. The scientists and many of the philosophers of the day were reluctant to accept this assessment. Newtonian dynamics matched natural appearances too closely. And it was predicting more and more phenomena every day. It surely must be a universal and necessary science of objective reality.

Immanuel Kant (1724-1804), who shared this conviction, also was convinced that Hume's argument was valid. He therefore took as premises the validity of Newtonian science and the validity of Hume's argument concerning induction. His formal problem was then to combine them in one consistent syllogism.

Hume himself, as Kant says in his *Prolegomena,* supplied the answer, namely that anticipation itself is responsible for the universality and necessity of scientific induction[1]. The anticipation is the presence in the mind of a priori forms which always shape sensible content in the same way. The result is regularity in the object of thought. The rational knower thus became the creator of meaning,

---

[1] Immanuel Kant, *Prolegomena to Any Future Metaphysic.*

the source which makes "nature" intelligible. This "Copernican revolution"[2] depended upon its premises and stood or fell with them. When scientists, at the turn of the century, no longer held that Newtonian principles were universal and necessary, it then fell.

But the *Critique*, even supposing the correctness of its premises, was inconsistent.[3] It could not explain, for one thing, how the knower could come to impose one structural form rather than another upon any given content of sense knowledge. This could not be because the a priori form was so determined; in that case it would not apply to any other content. Nor could it be because a particular sense content called for this form rather than another. This would ground the universality and necessity of natural law in the noumenal world itself, contrary to the contention of the *Critique* that it is grounded in the knowing subject. Both solutions led to the same impasse. The Kantian *Critique*, as he formulated it, could not explain how the a priori forms unified sense experience. For the post-Kantians, the only way to explain this was to ground both form and matter in subjectivity. The mind contains both and causes both. Hegel gave this theory its most nuanced expression. Kant's Pure Reason became Absolute Spirit objectifying itself in the world in order to return into itself becoming at last the Nous of Aristotle—Thought thinking itself.

This movement from science claiming universal and necessary knowledge to Absolute Spirit grounding all that is, in order to think itself is the essential dialectic in the growth of the modern mind and manifest Reason. The existential dialectic, such as it was exemplified in Kierkegaard, judging Hegel from his Christian consciousness of himself, manifested Faith and Will.

For this existential point of view, Hegel's system was false. Hegel thought that reason could grasp the meaning of existence. But the intelligibility of existence, for the Christian consciousness, is the impenetrable mystery of divine choice.

In this way, the fragmentation of reason and will in the modern mind finds expression—the consequence of late medieval

---

[2] Ed. See also page 19.

[3] Immanuel Kant's *Critique of Pure Reason*.

Nominalism. This fragmentation is also expressed in the tendency of Existential thought to use the negation of the scientific world view as the means for getting to the truth of being, as in Gabriel Marcel. Existence becomes known, not as rational, but as irrational. And this is the truth of being.

The contemporary philosophical consciousness, therefore, amalgamates an ontology—will— (based upon the rejection of the scientific mentality), and an epistemology—reason— (deriving from Kant's critique). The concern for language is a newer development which seems to be tending in the direction of overcoming the opposition of reason and will.

But the respect for science gave rise not merely to the endeavor to justify it, as in Kant, or to use it negatively to develop an existential ontology, but also to the endeavor to imitate it in all other forms of human thought. This is the sense of Positivism.

CHAPTER 3

POSITIVISM:

THE PRIME PHILOSOPHY OF THE MODERN MIND

Positivism attempts to conform philosophy to empirical science. Thus, it makes philosophy either a meta-empirical reflection upon the statements of science, or, as with Auguste Comte (1798-1857), it finds inductions and theories in philosophy which resemble those of science. And in all cases, it rejects the possibility of the universal upon which traditional philosophy has based its claim.

Thus traditional philosophy has argued that its subject is not as in this or that, but as in itself. Positivism denies the validity of this subject and allows only for the validity of the as in this or that of empirical science.

Empirical science never deals with heat "in itself" but only with heat in this or that body. The denial of the validity of the "in itself" is connected with the Nominalist interpretation of the universal, i.e., it is comparative, not absolute, and it is through diminution of being.

For medieval philosophy, as for the classical science, empirical science was a part of natural philosophy—that part whose arguments were no more than probable and whose theories could at best save the phenomena. This would follow from its subject: heat, e.g., as in this or that body. Its subject never was heat in itself. But in this conception, knowledge of what was in itself was the grounding of knowledge of what it was in this or that body. Grounding not as that from which phenomena could be deduced but as the whole which made the observed phenomena intelligible as parts in a whole. Positivism strips this away. There is no whole to serve this function. There is the pure atomism of the parts which are therefore not parts of a whole. The resultant picture is like a work of "art" whose aesthetic parts have no whole—it is radically unintelligible.

Thus, the classical picture gives heat in itself as the grounding of heat in this body. The properties of heat in itself are then got at by generalized induction and by relational analysis. The properties of heat in this or that body are got at by particular induction. Thus we say: What does heat have, not as in this or that body but as in itself? And we say: What does heat have as in this or that body or in all bodies? Thus in itself it is an accident. As in this or that body, it causes expansion. The relational grid is brought to the former question and answer, not the latter. For the former we ask the questions: Could it be the essence or the existence or a capacity or an operation?

Those theoretical insights are only probable and therefore always subject to change with further experimentation. In changing, it could always move closer to terminal truth, but never finally reach it. This is how the medieval philosopher would have understood the scientific evolution from Ptolemy to Newton and how, in fact, Bellarmine interpreted Galileo's thought. Greater exactitude in observations and measurements had made the modifying of approximative and probable explanations necessary. For the medieval philosopher, this necessity made empirical science scientifically inferior to a strictly demonstrative science such as mathematics, whose conclusions are not subject to correction through further experimentation.

But the medieval philosopher did not think that the probability of physical theory could be replaced by certainty. Its epistemological limitations made this impossible. In physics, as the Greek and the medieval thinker understood this, little can be known by demonstration. Nearly all knowledge in physics is necessarily approximative. Only the most generic knowledge is certain. By differentiating this generic knowledge, the philosopher can approach a demonstrative knowledge of specific intelligibilities.

By starting from the consequences of the specific intelligibilities of the "phenomena" the empirical scientist can also approach a true knowledge of specific natures. But the approach, in both cases, is through an infinite series of approximations which, because they are infinite, cannot be terminated. Nevertheless, in taking them, the two knowledges of physical things asymptotically approach specific intelligibilities. Holding this to be so, medieval philosophy, just as the ancient philosophy, did not separate the two approaches as radically as the modern does. It considered them rather as one science using two methods and two insights, the one sufficient and the other insufficient. The medieval philosopher thus postulated the unity of the discussion of the formal and material principles of changeable things and of the discussion of their mathematical laws.

During the post-Renaissance period, this unified conception gradually disappeared. When this happened, philosophy of nature was then divided radically from empirical science. Because of this, it eventually came to be neglected as invalid.

This did not occur at once. In the beginning, the older notion of the unity of the sciences prevailed. When Newton, for example, called his masterpiece the *Mathematical Principles of Natural Philosophy*, he implied that it was only part of a whole. And when Galileo, in writing up the results of his mechanical investigations, used scholastic terminology—speaking of the mathematical properties of natural and violent motion for bodies near the surface of the earth—he implied the same unity. The fact that his translators today have to render the terms "natural" as "free" and "violent" as "forced" shows how far they have come from his way of thinking. The separation to which this termino-logical change witnesses, first abstracted inductive empirical science from the unity of ancient physics and then gave it alone the name "physics."

One could argue that this was a small loss and that the consequent development of empirical science made adequate compensation for it. After all, while empirical science was tied to the older conception, it hardly made progress at all. But, once it was freed, it grew rapidly. The separation was therefore beneficial, and a reunion would not be desirable! In fact, this is not so. Empirical science has suffered from the separation. It has been left with a vacuum which, both the Kantian critique and Positivism, each in its own way, have tried to fill.

Positivism, in particular, might well be thought of in this context as an attempt on the part of abstracted "empirical science" to reverse the abstraction and fill the vacuum. With this unconscious purpose, Positivism took shape as a complement to empirical science. It imitated empirical methods. It rejected self-evident principles and accepted only empirical induction. From this induction it derived its own "metaphysical laws of nature," and from these laws it deduced empirical theories. For Positivism, this was the full range of valid knowledge. Any claim to knowledge lying outside of this was metaphysical in the pejorative sense. Positivism therefore made "empirical science" and the real convertible.

The recollection that metaphysics had apparently incorrectly interpreted many natural phenomena bolstered this conviction. "Metaphysics" had misunderstood the nature of the comets and Newtonian dynamics getting to the truth of the matter had corrected the misunderstanding. The Positivist was led to believe that in many other, if not all similar matters, empirical science would produce a similar correction. "Metaphysics" would then be clearly revealed for what it was—a false claim to know realty!

The counterclaim could of course be made that, if this were true, then Positivism itself must be invalid. No induction validates its postulates. They predetermine its outcome. Positivism might contend that it integrated the particular sciences and did not predetermine them. It therefore took its insights from them as a whole and did not deduce from itself any one of them. It was therefore the science of the whole, whereas the particular sciences were the independent sciences of the parts. It therefore claimed to be the finalizing science of all particular sciences, and thus the motivation of all particular empirical procedures, and for this reason, ultimate science.

Through the study of Positivism's evolution, it is easy to see how it came to make this sweeping claim. The teachings of Charles Fourier (1772-1834) represent an early state. Having been impressed with the sheer beauty and power of Newtonian mechanics, Fourier wondered if something similar could not be created in the field of social sciences. Newton had reduced the most complex motions to simple ones, and, from these, deduced the complex ones. Might not sociology do the same for the study of society?

In Newtonian dynamics, all the complexities of bodily motion were reduced to the laws governing the motion of atomic bodies relative to one another. Social science, if it were to be similar in logical structure to this, would have to find analogous social atoms and social laws. It seems to be able to do this. There seem to be social atoms—individual human beings—and "social laws"—"gravitational" forces which bind persons together in society. In Newtonian dynamics, the interaction of such forces tends toward equilibrium. In society, it should therefore tend toward peace (equilibrium). The society of his day, that Fourier felt had not reached this terminal point. Other forces were therefore disturbing it and thus keeping it from equilibrium as one planet in the Newtonian understanding of the solar system perturbs the motion of another. By studying such disturbances, the social scientist should be able to isolate their causes, and then possibly take corrective action. Sociology would be the Newtonian-style science whose application to society would produce universal peace and harmony.

Saint-Simon (1760-1825) thought that this picture of a Newtonian sociology should be generalized. If it were, then not only sociology but all other sciences too would become Newtonian in form. Their integration into a whole would replace traditional metaphysics. Taken as a whole, they would then say what legitimately can be said about the world.

Although Saint-Simon conceived this goal, he did not achieve it. Enthused by its attraction, Auguste Comte tried to do what Saint-Simon could not do, and actually bring it into being. If we assume, he reasoned, that the integration, organization, and unity of the particular sciences is the goal of unified science, then we must conclude that it is not one of them. It must therefore be a distinct discipline which assumes the role of traditional metaphysics. By the study of what this role must be, one could therefore determine what philosophy really is. It would have to be the consciousness of the synthetic whole of which the particular sciences are analytic parts. Newtonian methodology would have to be the means to produce this consciousness. Through this, the new science, in its perfect state, would have completely generalized certain principles which would comprehend all data. Traditional metaphysics could not do this. That is why metaphysics substituted the postulation of hidden causes—" theological" or "metaphysical" or "mystical" postulates—for terminal scientific inductions.

The "new science," in basing itself upon terminal scientific inductions, is positive, not negative. Only because of this, Comte was convinced, could it advance beyond particular sciences. He thought, obviously only an exhaustive study of all objective human thought could enable one to reach this final science. As final, it would therefore be the full consciousness of the human potential. This consciousness would then replace the traditional postulate of a God. *Positivism would become mankind's new religion.*

This was Positivism in its classical form. Even today, variations of this form continue to emerge in that they share the common conviction that the true philosophy must model itself upon empirical science, they are all one. Positivism is thus clearly a derivation from Newtonian dynamics. For it, whatever may be its form of reality is what corresponds to the actual or potential assertions of empirical science, and that alone exists which is "scientifically" intelligible.

Hume's attack upon the validity of induction obviously dealt this conviction a heavy blow. In the next chapter, we will study this and Kant's defense against it.

CHAPTER 4

HUME'S ATTACK UPON THE SUPPOSITIONS OF SCIENTIFIC METHODOLOGY AND KANT'S APOLOGETIC CRITIQUE

Positivism attempted to substitute scientific methodology for scholastic methodology by denying scholastic methodology to be self-evident a priori truths and admitting only propositions which arise from scientific induction. Bacon gave this position its classical expression. But other philosophers were not convinced, and thought, on the contrary, that science could not justify itself in this way and claim universality, necessity, and objectivity. This would be impossible unless science grounded its a posteriori inductions in a priori intuitions. This was Kant's contention which Hegel then qualified.

There were three steps in this dialectical interaction. In the first, Hume argued that scientific inductions did not produce universal and necessary objective knowledge, but only particular knowledge and subjective expectations. In the antithetical second step, Kant endeavored to restore objective universality and necessity to scientific inductions by postulating a priori forms in knowledge. In the synthetic final step, Hegel then argued that Kant's position could be sustained only if one grounded it in Absolute Spirit from which the world emanates so as to bring about the return of absolute Spirit into itself.

Hume had argued that induction, being finite (the number of observations is always limited), cannot produce an infinite result, i.e., a universal, necessary, and objective insight into "nature." What scientists were accustomed to call Newton's "universal laws of nature" were therefore no more than a finite collection of observations plus subjective expectations. Scientific knowledge, as no more than this, could not claim to be objectively universal and necessary.

This criticism obviously cut at the heart of "scientific" pretensions and, as a consequence, at the heart of those of Positivism too. After all, both claimed objective and true insight into nature. The scientists of Hume's time could not bring themselves to reject the accustomed view—and so to regard Newtonian dynamics merely as a system of subjective anticipations. Its success in solving complex physical problems and in predicting specific physical phenomena with great accuracy strengthened their reluctance. Yet, how could they then answer Hume? How could they show that Newtonian laws derive their objective universality and necessity from induction? They could not argue that this was self-evident. That would have restored scholastic a priori principles. Some other way out was needed. Kant provided such a way out.

He took as his point of departure two presuppositions: that Hume's criticism was valid, and that Newton's laws of dynamics were truly universal and necessary. He had then to find a theory to reconcile these presuppositions. It is important to stress that these are presuppositions whose justification is crucial to Kant's critique.

In the *Prolegomena to Any Future Metaphysics*, Kant relates how he came to his solution. He began by carefully considering Hume's analysis of causality. Following Locke's empiricist principles, Hume had argued that causality is a composed mental content made up of data provided by 1. sense and 2. relations added by the mind. Locke had claimed that this was the content of the concept of substance. Hume then applied the same to the concept of causality.

Kant thought that the notion could be further generalized. Perhaps all mental contents are similarly so structured so that in their formation the mind is always active. Deducing the consequences from this supposition, Kant first carefully distinguished Hume's contention that the causal concept contains the relation of expectation, from his (Hume's) conclusion that it is therefore not objective. He tried to find out, first of all, if this relation was universal, that is to say, if it exists in all contents of rational thought and not just in the concepts of science.

When he tested this possibility in the full range of human knowledge, he felt that it proved to be true. Everywhere anticipatory composition was apparently present. This discovery led him then to investigate its many forms. The result was the "Transcendental Deduction of the categories of Pure Reason."

To accomplish this "transcendental" deduction, he drew heavily upon preceding thought, attempting to reconcile Rationalism and Empiricism. He felt that he could justify Empiricism by grounding scientific induction, and Rationalism by making a priori forms of knowledge the grounding. Rationalism, which Leibniz exemplified, made all consciousness intellectual. Sensibility was defective intellection. The world was a world of self-knowing spirits.

Empiricism, which Locke and Hume exemplified, derived all mental content from sense data and relations added by the mind. It admitted no a priori intellectual insights of principles. Self-consciousness, such as it is, was a secondary phenomenon, arising from reflection upon a posteriori induction from sense experience.

The argument in favor of pure Leibnizian Rationalism rather than Empiricism was doubtless strong. In self-consciousness, the human person seems to have an intellectual knowledge which transcends sense consciousness. This makes some form of Platonism plausible.

Moreover, knowledge seems to be essentially intellectual and only peripherally sensible. It is true that, on this supposition, the problem of relating body to soul becomes difficult, but the dilemma seems not necessarily insoluble.

The argument for Empiricism, on the other hand, seemed equally strong. The incredible success of Newtonian dynamics, which was based upon induced laws from sense experience and could not be deduced from a priori intellectual insights, seemed to justify it.

Reflecting upon this, philosophers could therefore find good reason for admitting some validity to both opinions. When Kant began his investigation of Hume, this was his conviction. Reading Hume in this light, he though he saw the way out!

He began, therefore, by attempting properly to state the problem. That proper statement had to contain, first of all, the elements in common to both the Empiricist and Rationalist positions. Where they both agreed, they were both probably right. And both agreed that the problem was how to reconcile universal necessary knowledge with induction from singular sense experience. Seeing the problem in this way, and thinking that reconciliation was impossible, Leibniz simply suppressed one of the terms. He made sensible experience a confused intellection. Hume, seeing the problem in the same way, did just the opposite. He denied the objective validity of universal intellectual knowledge.

From the logical point of view, this opposition could be formally reduced to a syllogism, two of whose terms were given by the question itself properly stated and one of which would have then to be supplied by intellectual "imagination." Kant therefore took as a conclusion the statement: our knowledge, derived from sense experience, is universal and necessary.

Formally this yields the syllogistic structure:

> Major: MEDIUM is universal and necessary.
>
> Minor: Our knowledge, derived from sense experience, is MEDIUM.
>
> Conclusion: Our knowledge, derived from sense experience, is universal and necessary.

For completing this syllogism, that is to say finding the proper MEDIUM, Hume provided Kant the clue. In analyzing causality Hume had reasoned that, since it involves mental anticipation, it has no objective necessity or universality. For Kant this suggested a way out. If all our knowledge, and not merely knowledge of causality, involves "anticipation," and if the anticipation is stable, then, far from destroying objective universality and necessity, this would ground it.

By an investigation of each science in particular, Kant soon convinced himself that this was the case. Each one had, like physical science in the concept of causality, anticipatory forms. This is true even for mathematics. If this is so, then Reason is an active capacity which imposes a priori forms upon given sense data and thus produces its own object. The stability of the forms guarantees universality and necessity. Universal "nature" is the result. There is no noumenal content in mind but only a stable phenomenal one.

HUME'S ATTACK AND KANT'S CRITIQUE

The anticipatory relation, which, for Hume, destroyed true science, in fact creates and preserves it. The subjective and the objective are reversed. Prime importance has now to be given not to the noumenal thing in itself, to which previous epistemology had supposed that the mind must conform itself, but to the knowing mind which shapes nature. This was Kant's "Copernican Revolution." The sun (the self) now became the center of the universe and the earth (the "thing in itself") moved to the periphery.

Knowledge was therefore now active rather than passive. It shapes the manifold of sensation. The manifold of sensation justified Empiricism. The a priori forms justified Rationalism. Both were thereby reconciled.

This led Kant to distinguish the noumenal world of things in themselves from the phenomenal world of things in rational consciousness. Things in themselves are not known but only the phenomenal, or that which appears in rational thought. Newtonian science is therefore not noumenal but phenomenal. Nevertheless it is universal and necessary. And this makes it science.

With these conclusions Kant thought that he had justified the claim of empirical science to be universal and necessary. And he had done this by reconciling Rationalism and Empiricism in a higher unity of consciousness.

The post-Kantians showed that this solution was inconsistent. The correctives which they added to bring this about radically altered the character of the *Critiques* and restored something of the character of medieval scholasticism and Neo-Platonism. This was most marked in Hegel.

CHAPTER 5

HEGELIAN CORRECTIVES

Kant argued that all scientific knowledge depends upon a priori forms in the mind which shape "brute" sense experience. Exercising this activity, the mind assimilates data. The distinctions of the forms determine the distinctions of mental concepts. If this is so, then distinct forms create distinct sciences. Supposing geometry to be a distinct science, Kant tried to detect its distinct a priori form. He argued that this was space. And since arithmetic is distinct from geometry, he reasoned it too must have a distinct form. He argued that this was *time*.

In doing this, he recaptures the scholastic distinction between relation itself and its ground. Space and time were not relations but grounds. They were, therefore, forms of sensibility and grounds of relation. But space and time not only provide the basis for geometry and arithmetic, but also for all of the other sciences. This means that relation functions not only in physics, but also in all other sciences.

Thus, in arithmetic and geometry, what is done to the spatial and temporal continuum provides the terms of mathematical relations. And in physics, the same is true. In arithmetic, this should be division and then inversion of the division to generate numbers. But for Kant, numbers seem to be generated by addition of the unit. In geometry, it is division of the one given quantitative continuum. The first division in magnitude generates figures. The second division generates multiplicity. Thus, geometry is more unified than arithmetic. Thus it is multiplicity which grounds the categories, i.e., the many. Causality is the many as following one another in time.

It would seem that once the subject has been created by the structuring relation, it may be judged. Then conceptual distinction comes in. This explains the "is" form of judgment. On the other hand, since in practical knowledge the judgment comes first, the structural forms lie in judgment. It thus creates the object with these relational forms, and then it judges them.

Thus practical judgment is like a maker and makes them to be. Then they are. Thus judgment precedes in causality the actual existence of the content of conceptual consciousness. And all of the concepts involve a priori relational forms and they are synthetic a priori, i.e., they involve the putting together of the objectively distinct in the content of sense on the basis of a priori principles for relating. The particular structure in the relational composition comes from the a priori form to ground all relation. But it does this differently.

Thus, between the actual relations which are a priori in mind and the sensible data to which they apply, Kant posited grounds. Again, if the science of nature is, as most concede, still another distinct science, it must have its own a priori forms. And these are not in sensibility but in reason. Reason the higher principle transcending the lower forms needs them to supply the matter which they themselves shape. The result of this shaping we commonly call "nature." It is substance and accident, cause and effect, and so forth.

With this determination Kant felt he had grounded the sciences of mathematics and physics in a priori forms. He had still to ground traditional metaphysics. As in the former case, so in this case too, if this was still another valid science, as tradition held it to be, it had then to possess its own distinct a priori forms. The search for these led to peculiar difficulties.

Metaphysics, according to the traditional position, is a science of entities which transcend experience and therefore have no proper sensible analogues or representations. Kant could not therefore look to them to determine a priori forms as he had done with the sciences of mathematics and physics. This is clear from the question to which metaphysics naturally leads—how is it possible to have universal and necessary knowledge of the supra-sensible in contingent sensible matter? Kant found this question contradictory. There can be no sensible experience of the supra-sensible. This led him to rephrase it so as to remove the contradiction—can there be any relationship at all between the two? Or, if the supra-sensible cannot be a part of sensible experience, can it have any other relationship to it at all?

HEGELIAN CORRECTIVES

To say that it cannot, totally rejects the traditional conviction. To say that it can, implies a new relation which the tradition did not envisage. Kant took this position and determined that the new relation was not that of constructing objective contents, but that of finalizing them. When the mind constructs objective contents, it moves toward the supra-sensible as to an end. The supra-sensible is therefore that infinitely removed whole (never, as such, a content of sense experience) of which all particular mental constructions are parts. It supplies the ultimate unity of consciousness. Traditional metaphysics was therefore right in assigning to the supra-sensible some role in experience. But it was wrong in making this an objective content of thought rather than a goal. There is thus no true science of the world, the self, and God. The illusion that there is causes most of the difficulties which give rise to the great variety and conflict of philosophical opinions. The contribution of critical philosophy is to show that that illusion is the root of the problem, and at the same time, to show the way out.

In this way, Kant was able to reveal, to his own satisfaction, the true function and value of metaphysics. He could determine to what extent its traditional claims were valid and how necessary these claims were for sustaining the sciences of mathematics and nature. But he could also show where the claims of metaphysics were false. It could finalize mathematics and physics, but it could not prove the existence of God nor analyze the nature of the self or of the world. Having reached this conclusion, Kant felt that he had brought his investigation of the mechanism of rational knowledge essentially to a close.

He had justified Hume and Newton, conciliated Empiricism and Rationalism, grounded mathematics and related it to physics, and laid down *The Prolegomena to any future metaphysical considerations.* Speculative thought was now critically evaluated and understood. But there were problems in this critique which soon surfaced.[1]

---

[1] Problems formally the same as those which arose in the traditional treatment of final causality, although not known to be such by those who spotted them.

Idealists soon saw the crucial difficulties. They noted, first of all, that it is not consistent to say (and therefore not possible) within the Kantian critique that the noumenal world (of which we have no knowledge) is the cause of the phenomenal world (which is the Kantian object of our thought). Causality, by the conclusion of the critique, is a category of reason which applies only to a given sensible datum. The noumenal—the *Ding-an-Sich*—is not a given sensible datum (this was Kant's prime conclusion!). Therefore, causality cannot be attributed to the noumenal—that is, if the Kantian critique is to remain consistent.

But there is an even greater difficulty. The mind, by the critique, is supposed to apply general a priori forms to particular given matter. How can it do this? How can it determine which a priori form to apply to which given matter? This is the same formal problem which underlies the Greek and medieval conception of efficient causality and teleology. For Aristotle, its halting solution by Anaxagoras marked him out as the first rationalist, or as he put it trenchantly, as a "sober man among drunks," in comparison with his predecessors—a phrase dear to Hegel!

In essence, the problem is this. The mind, from the point of view of the critique, cannot act to impose any particular form upon given matter unless it is determined to do so. Where does it get the determination? If we say, from the applied for itself which has an inner relation to the given matter, then we destroy the form's universality. If, to save this, we say from the matter to which it is applied, then we destroy the critique. The forms are no longer purely a priori but are a posteriori—potentially imminent in the sensed object of experience. Therefore, we cannot say that the necessary principle of determination is in the noumenal, nor that it is in the content of sense experience, nor that it is in the a priori forms. Where else could it be then? Within the limits of the critique there is only one other place, and that is in the teleological wholes of metaphysics. It must be in the Ego, or the World, or God. If this is so, the Ego, or the World, or God posit both the matter and the form, thus at once bringing them into being and bringing them together. The Ideals of Pure Reason thus revealed themselves as not only the end of mental structuring, but also the beginning. This was, in short, the contribution of post-Kantian German Idealism.[2]

Fitche theorized that it must be the Ego which pours out the infinity of the phenomenal, and that it can do this for no other goal than itself. The Ego must do this to come into possession of itself, that is to say, to enter into itself in perfect and infinite self-consciousness. But this means that it must begin in the opposite state, namely in the state of total lack of self-consciousness. Where Kant has laid down the following schema, then:

World Ego	End-Whole
Categories	Forms of Rational Experience
Time - Space	Forms of Sense Intuition
Sensations	Matter: "Brute Sensation"

Fichte laid down this schema:

Ego	Position/Negation - Transitional
Categories	Formation - Rational
Time - Space	Formational - Sensible

The schema, of course, symbolize the relations involved, which are much more complex. But it represents, at least for Fitche, that they are all, grounded in the Transcendental Ego.

But where this proposal corrected one problem for Kant, namely that of finding the cause of the conjunction of the universal a priori forms with contingent matter in the flow of phenomenal experience,

---

[2] As one versed in classical and medieval teleology, the variations in this contribution which soon arose seem very familiar to me, but also, relatively, metaphysically naïve.

it immediately created another. It conceived of the "causality" of the Transcendental Ego in such a way as to render it important. If the Transcendental Ego does not already contain actually all that it grounds, then it cannot ground anything—i.e., it cannot act.

Schelling, recognizing this, corrected Fitche by postulating that the Transcendental Ego has perfect initial self-consciousness so that it can act. In this variation on the theme, Fichte comes close to the God of Aquinas. But the pouring out of the flow of the phenomenal by the Transcendental Ego is then a manifestation of the freedom of the Transcendental Ego. The phenomenal world becomes thereby rationally unintelligible. Reason cannot ground its existence.

This conclusion, which Kierkegaard took up, irritated Hegel. For Hegel, Fitche had created an Ego which *could* not act, and, Schelling, one which *would* not act (except, of course, freely). Neither was acceptable to him. He wanted an Ego which could act and would act, but from necessity, not freedom. Such an Ego had therefore to have, from the beginning, some self-consciousness, but it could not have the perfect self-consciousness postulated by Schelling. Therefore, it had to have an imperfect initial self-consciousness, and it had of necessity to pour out the phenomenal to achieve perfect terminal self-consciousness.

To the student of the history of philosophy, the formal similarity of this demand with that which classical thought made upon the final cause, both in ancient and medieval philosophy, is evident. And the student of history is therefore not surprised to find the many echoes of the tradition in the great Hegelian corpus, but least of all in the *noesis noeseos noesis* at the end of the *Encyclopedia of the Philosophical Sciences*.

Hegel himself again and again recognized this and, throughout all of his writings, he readily acknowledged it. With the positing of this "dynamic" Ego, as opposed to Fitche's and Schelling's perfect Ego, Hegel thought that he had reached the height of philosophical insight. From this vantage point, he thought he could also escape the problem of the noumenal, which had plagued the early post-Kantian commentators.

Rather than eliminate this entirely, as Fitche had done, he could reduce it also to the Transcendental Ideals. Out of dynamic Ego flow both the Phenomenology of the mind and the structure of nature as objective and noumenal. That being so, it seemed to him more appropriate to name this all transcending principle "Geist" rather than Ego, or World, or God.

In this choice, he was simply assimilating all the more the Neo-Platonic and Aristotelian tradition, so superficially at least, similar to his own thought. The Nous of Aristotle then became his fundamental Ideal of Pure Reason. The structure of empirical science, whose claims had been the beginning of all of this speculation, became, in Hegel's dialectic, the structure of all thought and of reality. The logic of probable statements in empirical science translates readily into the logic of thesis, antithesis, and synthesis.

The translation is most striking in Hegel's treatment of the principle of contradiction. The result of the schema of mounting triads from a beginning in pure Being to an end in the absolute return of the Spirit into itself (parallel with Neo-Platonic terminology) is striking and not by accident. Standing in the center point of rational consciousness, Hegel argues that the structure cannot go into infinity above or below. There must be an absolute beginning he therefore argues, and he identifies this with Being. And there must be an absolute end, and he identifies this with Nous, terminating the *Encyclopedia of the Philosophical Sciences* with the remarkable citation from Aristotle—the nearly prayer-like statement of the Stagirite on the life of the Nous.[3]

What was unique in Hegel's position, however, was his claim to adequate insight. The tradition admitted the same relational structure in reality as he did, although it would have said that he identified logical with ontological relations. But it denied that it understood much more than that the relations exist, claiming to apprehend their intelligibility only dimly. Hegel claimed to know it deeply. He claimed to know specifically why the Nous poured itself out in the world and in the empirical self. The why for him was thus

---

[3]Aristotle's Metaphysics, 1074b34, *noesis noeseos noesis*.

accessible to reason as it was not for Aristotle and Aquinas. Nothing "as in a mirror darkly."[4]

Kierkegaard found the claim irreconcilable with Christian consciousness. Schelling's philosophy of freedom, which he heard exposed in 1841 in Schelling's Berlin lectures, was reconcilable. Hegelianism was hubris. Christian self-consciousness was human humility which seemed to him correctly to stress the essential freedom of God with respect to the world and the empirical self.

He allowed for a Christian understanding of man as unable by his own resources alone to escape his human limits. Philosophy cannot "bring the concept to piety." Piety brings the "concept" to philosophy and tells philosophy what it is.

We have now run the range of a certain limited history of Western European human self-consciousness—from the emergence of the modern mind in the post-Renaissance period to critical reflections upon this in Kant, Fichte, Schelling, and Hegel. In the next chapter, we will try to put this limited range in the larger perspective.

---

[4] Cf. Saint Paul, 1 Cor. 13:12.

CHAPTER 6

REFLECTIONS AND ASSESSMENT

We have laid out what we consider to be the essential steps in Hegel's thought. We will now investigate their ultimate sense. Reflection upon the dynamism of empirical science is a useful way for doing this. This is similar to Baruch Spinoza's reflection upon the dynamism of Cartesian philosophy.

Spinoza first laid down the goal toward which Cartesian philosophy was moving. That gave it its terminal sense. And this gave sense to each intermediate step. In the same way, the ultimate goal or the movement of thought which Kant and Hegel embody gives sense to their speculations. Kant's point of departure, as he lays it down in the *Prolegomena to Any Future Metaphysics*, are the suppositions that Newtonian inductions are universal and necessary and that Hume's argument concerning induction is correct. This leads to the conclusion that the universality and necessity is not from induction, i.e., not a posteriori but a priori.

I

What could be the source of this? Hume had claimed that the supposed universality and necessity were subjective expectation not objective fact. Kant converted this into *a priori forms in the mind.*

The logical difficulties in this position then led to the correctives of Fichte, Schelling, and Hegel. This is one sweep in modern thought. The broader sweep, which contains this one, is that of the Nominalistic late medieval characteristic of all modern thought which comes to it from Suarez through Descartes and gives context to the movement from Kant to Hegel. The still broader sweep reaches back into antiquity through the philosophical tradition antithetical to Nominalism.

One could therefore divide this full range of Western philosophical consciousness into the two lines of Nominalism and Anti-Nominalism. This latter would include, as its most important components, the currents of Platonism and Aristotelianism. And this full range of western philosophical consciousness must then be seen as having its roots in practical social action.

From beginning to end, this is its matrix. Conscious of this, Aristotle lays it down in the first book of the Metaphysics that practical action comes first and speculative contemplation, second. Human beings seek first of all to live and then, when this is assured, to contemplate.

This does not mean that the contemplative is inferior to the practical. It means only that the practical comes first in the order of generation. In fact, it can be shown that the practical inevitably leads to the contemplative, that it knows that the contemplative is higher, and that the contemplative is the perfection of the practical. Moreover, since it is the *natural* perfection of the former the practical has no choice but to move toward it. Every nature necessarily seeks its perfection!

That contemplation is the perfection of man becomes only gradually clear, and does not, at first, even seem probable. But the pursuit of the practical eventually makes this clear. It can occur only in the matrix of society. Man can provide adequately for himself only through social cooperation. But this then inevitably leads to leisure and leisure pushes man to contemplation. This, of course, occurs only in societies which manage to provide the quality of leisure which supports contemplation. And they are few. Most societies, as we know of them through history, never manage to achieve the natural ideal. In the ancient world Greek society alone closely approached it in many ways, with the result that the Greek contribution to culture and philosophy stands out among all others. Nevertheless, it can be argued, the movement from the practical to the speculative is natural to the human mind however rarely it may in any way be achieved.

II

We have now considered in essential detail the steps leading to Hegel. We will investigate their significance in the light of the end result. Kant's *Critique of Pure Reason* defends the position that Newtonian laws are universal and necessary by grounding them in a priori forms of reason. These, applied to the content of sensibility, produce similarity in the objective contents of reason. This is scientific experience through which sense knowledge becomes continuous with reason. Reason thus touches two extremes. The lower extreme is its perception of the objects of external sense, and the higher its insight into a priori principles. The lower extreme is singular materiality, whereas the higher is generic universality.

Thus, as the infra-rational passes up this range, it moves from the singular and practical to the universal and impractical. At its final term in the science of metaphysics, it then becomes absolutely universal and totally impractical. Therefore Aristotle says, metaphysics is the highest and most desirable knowledge, but at the same time, the least useful. All lower human knowledge is less universal and more practical. This is true of "empirical science," which was Kant's initial concern.

In this way the practical gives rise to the pursuit of the speculative. In the growth of human society practical knowledge thus comes first, and speculative knowledge arises only when practical knowledge feels an inner necessity to go beyond itself. Hence by the law of natural growth, surprising as this is to the average man who does not believe that he ultimately seeks pure contemplation, practice leads to speculation. The good of others becomes a concern for a human being when he discovers that he cannot take care of himself without also caring for others. This teaches him that he is naturally social, and he then begins to develop his social desires. More complicated needs then arise which impel him to seek more sophisticated forms of satisfaction. To the extent that social organization supplies these it also suggests other needs of even greater complexity. Through the knowledge that these are in the mind, the mind begins gradually to learn more and more about itself—it is the source of such wants. Through this realization it comes to know the richness and depth of its own being, which contemplation alone ultimately satisfies. In this way, it seeks and finally reaches contemplative wisdom.

At the lowest stage of social organization human beings unite in cooperative societies to provide for immediate material needs. Their success in achieving this goal leads to new possibilities. Thus society grows and with its growth, human beings discover their potentialities.

It was the hope of the Greeks that in the polis these potentialities would be fully realized. They thus saw the polis as the locus of the full development of the human potential, i.e., the place where a human being discovers fully what it is to be human.

Political society, in this way, develops from economic. The development causes new desires, and these require new social forms to satisfy them. Through this process human beings come to learn what they are. In this way human practical interests give rise to the desire for contemplation.

In his first judgments man grasps only his animal needs, and in his first words expresses only them. But once he has grasped and expressed these and their relationship to simple economic society, he then advances to the grasp of specifically human needs—the more abstract and universal good and political society which satisfies them. He then expresses this loftier consciousness in the myths.

In this evolution of human thought, as Aristotle shows in the first book of the Metaphysics, that the myth has a precise function. It rationalizes practical needs. But this then makes human beings wonder, and thus science and philosophy arise. The myth thus gives rise to new desires and these require new social forms. In this way society undergoes continual change. And through this, human beings come to learn what they are.

Although the scientist is sometimes aware of this, he often fails to recognize its significance. Mistakenly, he sees his thought as the rejection of the myth rather than its natural development. He thus loses the fertile and illuminating insight that the myth, by fastening upon the potential subject of empirical science, readies it for scientific actualization. Without this preparation science would never come into being. Man can question nature meaningfully only when he first understands the myth!

The mythmaker is therefore the father of the scientist and the philosopher. He must first be convinced on practical grounds that there is a God who rewards or punishes men for his acts and thus makes human life intelligible. Only on this basis can he then seek similar intelligibility in all other things. In this way alone is the wonder possible which originates science. Therefore in the growth of human knowledge the myth comes first, and it is its insight which leads man to search for the intelligibility of nature.

Once man has found the imperative that the myth precedes science in theory, he has passed to the second step in empirical science. Having through observation of singulars discovered these regularities and stated them as laws, he now in theory postulates probable explanations. The myth again helps him to do this; it is clearly again the origin of science. In this way myth controls the entire development of speculative knowledge. Although, as it becomes more general it also becomes less practical. Nevertheless, it maintains a connection still with the practical myth. So it is that human knowledge develops a full range from the practical to contemplation.

Since this order of knowledge is so, it follows that the subjects of practical knowledge are potentially the subjects of speculation. And so the subjects of the myth become successively the subjects of science and philosophy, first of nature and then finally of metaphysics. And metaphysics then, as the Neo-Platonists stressed, recaptures the myth from a different point of view, conforming to its convictions.

III

In light of the practical to speculative process of knowledge one can evaluate Kant's thought as, in essence, a response to the denial that empirical science is continuous with a higher metaphysics. While first supporting this denial, Kant ended up by attributing metaphysical properties to science. This was in effect what he did when he postulated a priori forms, but when he postulated the Ideals of Pure Reason as goals, he reintroduced metaphysics by the back door. Hegel demonstrated this by showing that the Ideals could not function purely and simply as goals. Hegel then, in his turn assigned them a grounding role which caused Kierkegaard's faith reaction.

In the growth of philosophical consciousness which had this modern result, the mythmaker was the origin. He mediated the passage from myth to science and philosophy. And whereas in the myth man was the subject of interest, in science and philosophy everything not man as well as man himself gradually became the subject. So also it came about that, where human beings on the myth level of thinking attributed everything to intelligent and free causes—man and God—on the level of scientific thinking human beings have tended to attribute all to blind necessity or chance.

The moderns simply exploited the possibilities of the myth and then jettisoned it. But still, the subject of the myth was essential for the creation of the subject of empirical science. That subject was the intelligibility and the goodness or evil of human action. In the myth we are concerned with human action in its social context. What human beings intend to do and what they *actually do* and whether this is good or evil and should be rewarded or punished. The myth thus gives us a notion of who and what a human person is. Science and philosophy simply extrapolate this interest gradually to all other things so that they then become for the thinker not things to be used, but things in themselves. But it is clear that this extrapolation depends upon the prior conception of what a human being is. This, given first in the myth, grounds science and philosophy, and so it permitted the philosopher to ask:

1. "What is substance in itself?"

2. "What is motion in itself?"

3. "What is being in itself?"

This was wonder, and out of wonder philosophy grew.

Thus the predecessors of the early Greek philosophers were, as Aristotle says, theologians. That is to say they were myth narrators for whom the knowledge and intentions of God or the gods were the ultimate basis of meaning. And the first genuine philosopher was the man who postulated that change in itself demands an ontological principle of identity in changeable things. Thales thought that this identity principle must have the character of water. There are two affirmations here:

1. that there is an ontological identity principle in all changeable things, and

2. that it has something of the character of fluidity.

The first affirmation persisted in Greek thought, but the second did not.

The subsequent growth of early Greek philosophy was a series of modifications of the second statement. The "atomism" of Democritus was an aberration. The Eleatics developed the implications of the presence of the term "being" in this growth, and thereby moved directly into metaphysics. In this way Greek philosophy came rapidly and profoundly to evolve the philosophical notions of subject of change: efficient cause of change, its final cause, the unity of matter, form, being, and the function of intelligence and will. With this profound notion of the analogy of being the unity of being is the unity of the relational.

Aristotle brought this theoretical development to its most profound term. He laid bare the essence of metaphysics, the only self-conscious science that not only is identical with its object but also with itself. First philosophy, or simply theology as he termed it, shares more than any other human knowledge in the divine in its self-consciousness. Hegel paid tribute to this, at least in part, by his famous last statement in the *Encyclopedia*. [1]

Kant's major contribution to modern thought was to begin again, unconsciously and however inadequately, to restore this insight to modern thought. His Ideals of Pure Reason were a recognition that the atomistic fragmentation of knowledge and being in modern philosophical theory, made knowledge impossible and being

---

[1] Georg W. F. Hegel, *Encyclopedia of Philosophical Sciences Part One*.

unintelligible and valueless. The Baconian and the Humean fragmentations of logical conclusions from premises rendered scientific knowledge for him impossible. This was to show, in a limited way, that the end of it all is return into self and diversity in identity. Kant was really arguing to the rooting of all in the identity of self-consciousness, as Hegel quickly and accurately perceived.

The a priori forms whether of Sensibility or of Reason, were simply projections of identity and of the return into self. Their relation to the Ideals of Pure Reason would soon in the hands of post-Kantian Idealists reveal this. They noted that an end has a twofold function, to lead to a goal by serving as a guide, and by doing this, to realize itself. Kant saw the necessity of the former, but not of the latter. In other words, he did not see that the Ideals of World, the Self, and God not only finalize rational thought, but also realize themselves through it, and that this is their true purpose. Fichte, Schelling, and Hegel saw this deeper purpose.

Kant therefore drew the minimal conclusion from the evidence. The maximum conclusion would have been the restoration of metaphysics. It was to the credit of the post-Kantians that they, at least partially, saw this. By the corrections which they made in the Critical Philosophy of Kant they recaptured lost doctrines of the Aristotelian-Platonic tradition. They thus came to accept, as had the Neo-Platonists before them, that human reason is to be explained by pure intellection—the lower by the higher and objective science by the return of the spirit into itself. To this extent, they also recaptured the thought of Thomas Aquinas.

In the light of these considerations the contributions of Kant and his disciples to the philosophy of the modern period was the determination of what empirical science supposes in order to exist at all. His was the contribution that philosophy had to make in order to relate to its milieu. But it contained certain conceptions which Kierkegaard could not accept. This was the cause of his revulsion.

Before proceeding further with an analysis and evaluation of that reaction we must now make a more penetrating analysis of the goal of rational thought. This will help us better to situate the thought of the post-Kantians, and also to understand the significance of

REFLECTIONS AND ASSESSMENT

Kierkegaard's rejection of them. In the next chapter, that will be our purpose.

CHAPTER 7

FURTHER REFLECTIONS AND ASSESSMENT

In the last chapter, we made a partial assessment of what was at play in the movement of the modern mind. It could be thought of as a repetition of the movement from myth and philosophy in antiquity to the myth/history conflict. Both mythical thinking and philosophical thinking led the ancients to the conviction that what should be happening in human history was not in fact happening.

The myth took this understanding of what should be happening and what was good or bad in human action from the presuppositions of action. Philosophy took what should be happening from the metaphysical study of nature. Both agreed that human action does not conform to the prescriptions of action nor to the postulates of human nature.

This is, in essence, the so-called "myth/history conflict." If history is understood to be the concrete actions of the human person, then it is clear from experience that these do not conform to the norms of either action or speculation. This perception makes human action unintelligible both from a practical and a speculative point of view. The effect upon action is to cripple it. The effect upon speculation is likewise crippling.

With respect to action, there is a human tendency to rejection of myth values, and with respect to speculation a tendency to skepticism. Total rejection of all values is not possible. There would then be no action at all, which is to say that there will not be the action of rejection either. Likewise with skepticism, total negation of all thought principles being itself a thought action is impossible.

Thus it is not possible to act except under the imperative of will—good is to be done and pursued, and evil is to be avoided.[1] Even suicide, which seems to be an act of self-hatred, is necessarily an act of self-love. In suicide the means to the end of self-love are wrong, but they are thought to be good and only for this reason pursued. For the same reason, the principle of contradiction can be negated in speech but not thought away, just as no conception can be entertained except as a contraction of being.

The history of human thought and action reveals an oscillation between admitting the conflict and perhaps bowing to it as the inevitable human condition and attempting to overcome it by thought or by action. This is, of course, an oscillation outside of the order of faith and purely within the order of human nature. The oscillation is due to both the despair of human nature to be able to do anything about the situation and to its sudden confidence that it has the resources within it to overcome the difficulty. Thus, there arise periods in human thought when science, for example, feels that it has the way out. Or philosophy sometimes becomes confident that it has the answer. Then again, there are periods when the confidence falls away and when a mass despair seems to be the order of the day.

In science, in the seventeenth to the nineteenth centuries, there was more of this confidence than there is now. And in the Hegelian philosophy of the nineteenth century there was perhaps the most incredible conviction in all the history of philosophy that to understand the meaning of history and the basic structuring principles of reality and thought was at hand. The Hegelian confidence arose from confidence in science, a position which Hegel accepted from Kant. But with the collapse of that confidence in the scientific world itself in the early 1900s at the turn of the century it was difficult to maintain it in the world of philosophy. Hegelianism then came to seem pure arrogance and a sort of irrational mysticism.

Outside the realm of science this lack of confidence in Hegelian philosophy had already occurred to Kierkegaard standing within the context of faith. Judging Hegelian philosophy by his Christian consciousness he found it totally incompatible. From this standpoint,

---

[1] Cf. Aquinas, ST, I-II, 94.2.

and not from within the context of philosophy itself, he had to reject it.

When philosophers came to share the loss of confidence in science existentialism arose. Existential philosophy had many points of resemblance with the thought of Kierkegaard, but, of course, it got to those points through a different point of view.

CHAPTER 8

THE DYNAMISM OF THOUGHT AS THE ULTIMATE SENSE OF KANT AND HEGEL

To situate Kantian and post-Kantian thought in the history of philosophy, it is necessary to investigate in detail the teleology of rational thought. The reflections of Kant upon the function of the Ideals of Pure Reason were a partial contribution to this investigation. The reflections of Hegel on the origins of thought and reality in the self-realizing spirit were a further step in this direction. Both Kant and Hegel led to theoretically situating empirical science between totally objective experience and self-consciousness.

In this placing of empirical science there was more than a little truth. The fact that it apparently fits the phenomenology of knowledge and even is necessary to explain it shows this to be so. As we have seen, in Phenomenology there is a growth of consciousness from the practical to the speculative.

There is also within the practical and speculative spheres in total self-consciousness a common teleology. Both spheres end in self-possession. The practical moves to self-possession through custom, law, and virtue. Speculation moves to it through growing insight in empirical science and philosophy. At the term both practical and speculative spheres become the same, and for that reason it has the qualities of both. This fact, discoverable through tracing the interconnections of both and their final end, is what Kant showed to be true for the justification of empirical science and what Hegel and the other post-Kantians showed to be true for all contents of consciousness whatsoever.

It therefore follows that rational consciousness is bracketed between two determinable boundaries: on its lower, sense consciousness bounds it; and on its higher, pure intellection. In that they are simple insights the upper and lower boundaries are similar.

Reason, which is in between, is complex. But one can say of its complexity that it comes out of simplicity and aims at simplicity. It comes out of the total objectification of sense knowledge and aims at the total subjectivization of intellectual self-possession.

Because of this common rooting and common term, the phenomena of rational consciousness, although distinct on that level, nevertheless are intimately related. So it is, that virtue, although not the same thing as science, is necessary for science. And the good life affects contemplation. Aristotle and Plato, sharing this conviction, thought that true wisdom was incompatible with vice; and that the function of virtue was to control the imagination and the passions, in other words the life of the senses, so that contemplation could take place. Vice has a braking effect upon contemplation so that one cannot move very far toward speculative self-possession if one is at the same time moving toward practical estrangement. Probably this was the core intuition of Socrates when he equated knowledge with virtue and thought therefore that virtue can be taught. It was probably also Spinoza's core intuition when he compared sin with speculative error and made the goal of his metaphysics the moral goal of happiness. So, in his Ethic he tried to show that the Cartesian method for eliminating speculative error was an ethical method for producing beatitude.

There is a long tradition in philosophy which holds that the return of the spirit into itself is the goal of rational life—both speculative and practical. As to whether this goal is achievable in the present life philosophers have differed. Plato apparently thought that it was. Aristotle certainly thought that it was not, and that actually to achieve it even in a life to come is to become divine—a possibility which he did not think plausible. Others thought that, though it was achievable beyond this life, it would not then be compatible with survival of personal identity that it would occur through absorption into a higher consciousness of the whole or some such other entity.

The Empiricist thought current in philosophy resists this conviction, and grounds its resistance in the obvious origin of rational consciousness in sensation. This leads it to deny a priori reasoning to be valid and to deny that the goal of rational consciousness is self-possession. With respect to this denial, the critique of Kant, although narrowing itself upon empirical consciousness, was lethal. It was a demonstration that empirical consciousness cannot stand alone but must depend upon subjectivity. This implies, as Hegel was to point out, upon the return of the spirit into itself.

But, together with this demonstration, Hegel also showed that it is an exaggeration to imagine that the return of the spirit into itself is complete from the beginning, or in other words, that there is no growth in consciousness or in nature. In principle, this is what Leibniz had said. His conception of the monads at all events made their growth in consciousness problematical. Hegel in contrast to this, and in the spirit of Aristotle, took the middle course—the goal is self-possession.

The various levels of consciousness are possible only because they participate in the supreme level of self-possession and aim to transcend themselves in it. But their beginning is not in perfect self-consciousness. Of necessity they grow toward this from an imperfect initial stage. Hegel differed in this from Fichte and Schelling, who for him made that growth either impossible or unnecessary.

In this same spirit, Aristotle developed a parallel doctrine on the nature of virtue, which is to say, on the nature of the good act. He saw this act as rooted in animality but aiming at intellectual return into self. Through it a man comes to dominate himself, that is to say not merely to exercise a certain discipline over himself, but by doing the good act to possess himself. Plato, on the contrary, conceived of virtue as purgative, that is to say as getting a man outside of his body and making him conscious that he transcends animality, and therefore is not defined in terms of it. Thus in the good act, Plato stressed exteriority, whereas Aristotle stressed interiority.

But what Plato and Aristotle stressed was a difference within a basically identical position, namely that the end of it all is self-possession. The Empiricist who rejects this must deny that the good act is a participation in self-possession or self-consciousness. He must therefore attempt to give it value in itself without reference to self-possession—as the Positivists attempted to do for empirical science. And, just as the Kantian critique of speculative knowledge was an effort to show that what the Positivists tried cannot be, so a parallel critique of practical action would show that there too it cannot be that the good act has value in itself.

One could say that the most profound contribution to philosophy of the so-called post-Kantian Idealists, and particularly of Hegel, was the recapturing of an ancient conviction that all is rooted in absolute self-consciousness. The Hegelian version of this insight was not a simple repetition of the ancient one, but it was *essentially* the same. The student of Hegel's works knows how deeply he was himself convinced of this and how it made him view his own thought as an assimilation not only of the modern mind through the explication of its presuppositions, but also of the medieval and the ancient conviction.

Sin and error, the ethical and the speculative, therefore take their sense, in the final analysis, from the perfect return of the spirit into itself. A phenomenological analysis of either shows that this is so. From the metaphysical point of view sin is a rational phenomenon which must be referred to full humanity in order to be understood. And this means that it must be referred to the full return of man into himself or the full possession of man's being by his own intellect. The endeavor to achieve this possession is necessarily the motive in any human action. Sin is not a movement contrary to this. No such movement is possible. Man has no choice but to seek to know and love himself. But he can fail in the movement toward this end by taking the intermediate as the end. This in essence constitutes sin. Sin is in effect an action which attempts to make the means the end. It is the acceptance of the part as the whole. This is a refusal to possess the whole self, it is active alienation from the true self. Its theological component precludes a proper relationship to God.

In this conception evil consists in identifying the means with the ultimate end. This is parallel to the speculative "sin" of taking empirical science as self-sufficient. In both cases, the intermediate is invested with the properties of the terminal. The consequence of this way of viewing the situation is that one comes to see the moral act as rooted in the absolute. The moral act is an attempt to seize the absolute through action. Speculative insight is an attempt to seize it through knowledge. We reject the purely temporal interpretation of our actions in our resistance to death. We reject the same interpretation of our science by our insistence that it be grounded in being. The phenomena are parallel. The fear of being in error is rooted in the same cause as the fear of death.

It is in becoming conscious of both fears that we grasp our grounding in the absolute. This was the conviction of Hegel and of Kant. Sin is therefore possible, as is error, only because we can mistake the means for the end. Because we move to a terminal self-possession through intermediate stages which share in it, we can sin, and we can err. How this happens can be graphically represented as in Figure 8.1

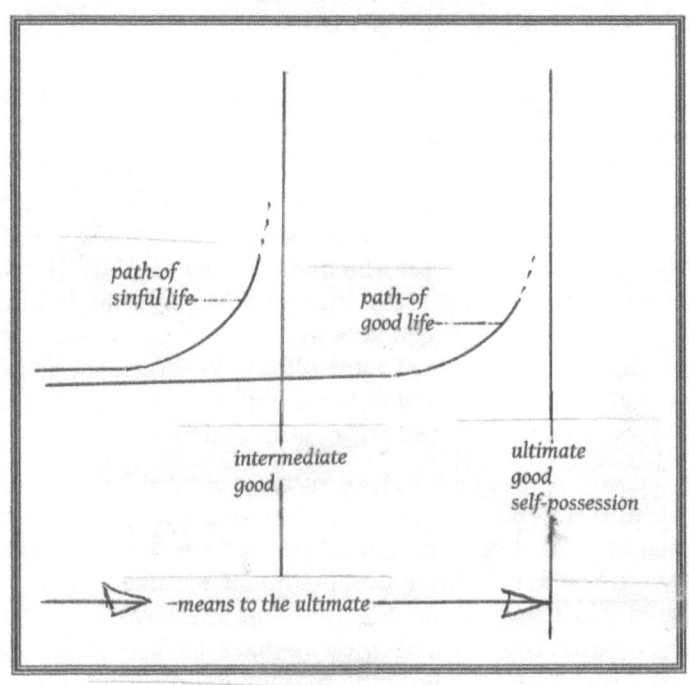

Figure 8.1 STATES OF LIFE

Envisage a sequence of moral actions or of intellectual perceptions as a movement toward a goal such that the movement must always go forward but never finally touch the goal. Using Zeno's paradox, we can quantify this situation. At any point of the movement, we may take a half step closer to the goal. It is clear that this procedure will result in an infinity of sequential movements short of the goal. It is clear also that the same can be said with respect to any intermediate position. From where one now is, it would take an infinity of steps to get to the given intermediate.

This is the situation for the sinful life. It moves always toward the true ultimate, but also toward an intermediate which it identifies with the ultimate (judging by appearances). And, therefore, through choice, it puts the self in opposition to the self. It thereby creates alienation within the self. This feeling, phenomenologically analyzed, reveals the truth of this representation.

The truth is revealed through the explication of the grounds of choice or of action in general. Suppose that true self-possession was the ultimate end of human action. If this is represented by a line perpendicular to a horizontal line representing the movement toward it, then the movement of the good life is asymptotic to the line representing true self-possession, and the movement of the evil life, asymptotic to an intermediate perpendicular. The sinful life is further distinguished from the good life in that it multiplies the intermediates since it can actually attain them, at least in principle, and thus it tends toward multiplicity. Whereas the good life tends toward unity. This is what puts the self in opposition to the self in the evil life. This is a possibility for rational action.

Therefore the very nature of the rational being creates such a possibility for him. Since his self-possession is divided between an initial imperfect one and a final perfect one, the rational spirit must move toward the final possession. This need then creates the possibility of alienation, of feeling that one's own choice makes one's nature (one chooses the intermediate as the end), and also the possibility of seemingly being many persons. Thus Thomas Aquinas can say that the movement to virtue is the movement to simplicity and that the movement to vice is a movement to multiplicity.

The opposition of self to self that can thus occur for the rational being is experienced as guilt. The very essence of guilt is the experience of this opposition. It is the experience that what should be is not. But this could exist only if there really was a *should* (ultimately the possession of the true self) and if choice could do nothing about it. The factual experience of guilt and the factual experience of the impossibility of removing it by any human device is therefore itself (when analyzed) indicative of the situation. It implies, in other words, the rational situation of movement between an imperfect possession of self and a perfect possession with the possibility of choice with respect to the means but not with respect to the end.

If, on the other hand, guilt is interpreted as not the consequence of failing to move properly to a true ultimate self-possession, but as choice needlessly at odds with itself then a number of conclusions may be drawn. One may, for example, regard the feeling of guilt as the consequence of choice itself and not the ground of choice. This would then be because one chooses with respect to an end which is an illusion or impossible or in no way necessary. In this case choice makes human nature such as it is. One could also conclude from this that, aside from the choice, there is no ought—that it is the choice itself which is projecting the ought. Thus there is no value aside from choice. One can see in this conception of the situation the basis for Nihilism, for Nietzsche's *Ubermensch*, and for the claim of some variations of Existentialism that choice is the essence and that it makes "nature."

Of course, the most immediate argument against choice itself projecting the ought, is that, if it were the case, then choice should be able to remove the conflict and the feeling of guilt. There have been no successful suggestions about how to do this. All theories—those also in the fields of depth psychology, political science, and economics, insofar as they impinge upon the guilt experience—have failed.

They therefore proceed from hope not from verifiable success. And some of the theories or ideologies have led to greater human suffering and greater sense of guilt, not to the alleviation of the pain. Some who have been more or less convinced that this is the case have then come to the conclusion that the only real choice is suicide. This they see as the necessary metaphysical and psychological consequence of sinful life—if it lasts long enough for the factors which are always present in it to play themselves out to this final end.

Something similar to this situation arises also in the parallel life of growing knowledge. There too, one may artificially introduce what is really an intermediate goal as an ultimate, and there too, when this is done, experience the effects noticed in the moral life: the sense of alienation from self, of division of personality, and of resultant frustration. In the moral life these reveal themselves by gradually suppressing motivation and replacing it with despair; in the speculative they reveal themselves by dimming intelligibility and replacing light with darkness—wherein the object seems to disappear, to move progressively, not toward intellectual clarity, but toward its privation. And this is truly what is happening! For just as in the practical movement of life where the growth of virtue follows a path which brings the will more and more into the proximity of the god of the quiet, or rest, which is happiness; so in the speculative, the growth of knowledge follows one which brings the mind more and more into the proximity of the absolutely intelligible, or perfect self-knowledge. And when this is not the case, and they fail to follow such paths, deviating from them, then the spirit seeking after goodness finds evil and the spirit seeking after light finds the dark.

The "sinful" speculative life has this peculiarity not found in that which is ordained to truth: it involves a disintegration of consciousness. This is manifested in the tension it experiences between the truth and that goal which it arbitrarily sets for itself. The thinker, moving along its path, looks ahead to its clearly indicated term. But, in seeing this, he also sees behind it the true goal—only vaguely there and yet solely responsible for his urge to know. As the difference between these two becomes more and more evident to him his inner tension also mounts, manifesting to him his state of disintegration wherein he sees himself as a divided speculative ego. The inevitable result of this is despair and darkness.

Not that it is possible for the speculative mind to achieve the pure non-possession of self, that is to say, a condition diametrically opposed to its return into its own essence. This is metaphysically absurd; just as pure subsistent evil, as with any pure privation, is absurd. All such privations can exist only in an impure state as accidents of the otherwise substantially good and true. And thus the movement to self-alienation exists only by being grafted onto that which terminates in genuine self-possession, causing this latter to unfold in such a way as never actually to get beyond an intermediate step. In so doing it always seeks the true end, it always desires this true end. But at the same time it renders its attainment impossible, clouding the spirit of man and throwing upon it the peculiar hue of human frustration; making him seek self-alienation, self-destruction, and self-disintegration rather than self-possession. It makes him to move speculatively not to full truth, but to its privation, not to intelligibility, but to irrationality. It causes a guilt and a hurt in the speculative mind akin to that which sin causes in the moral sphere.

This occurs for the reason that such intermediate goals are achievable. And if they are factually achieved, they then push the mind to discover new and different intermediates to function as its next goal. For none of the intermediate goals will allow the mind finally to come to rest. Every one of them being, of its very nature, not a term, but a point of transition to the beyond that once it is reached drives the mind ahead. Each one of them thus satisfies a temporary urge, a passing desire of the spirit, and in a distinct way, for they are contrary one to the other. Therefore they cannot all co-exist in the mind in the intermediate stage of its development short of self-possession where they would be united in a higher way. But the spirit desires that they should be united, and because they do not the spirit falls into a profound despair, knowing the futility of its quest.

This is actually what has happened in the progress of modern thought. For as it moved away from its point of origin, it did so under the supposition of empirical or dialectical thought as its ultimate goal and the only true term as the rational process. It thought that by achieving this goal it would be rendered happy. But as it proceeded to act upon this presumption, it became more and more aware of its conflict with the profound desires of the mind. Because of these profound desires the mind was thus committed to frustration and failure. This it began to see was a speculative "mortal sin" by which it set for itself an improper goal. Its logical next step was to erase the "sin" by embracing the belief in the creativity of its own processes, the negation of God in the moral sphere—thus to remove the sense of guilt by destroying the conviction of a different true ultimate. But such a move, although necessary and inevitable for it, could offer it no solution since the soul had no power to make it. Its limited and created mind could not reject the truth of self-possession by which ultimately it would recognize itself for what it was, a creature, and love itself as such, that is to say, love God above itself as its Maker.

Once the modern mind erected dialectical science into its final goal this degeneration was inevitable, and it had gradually to sense that its movement was toward obscurity rather than light, toward privation rather than possession. And yet it could not accept privation without profound melancholy over the division of its spirit, for this latter instead of tending to that unity which should characterize its term developed a speculative schizophrenia, a sense of double personality. Like the sinner of Saint Thomas it became another, and in fact many other persons, thereby losing the inner sense of cohesion which it had possessed in the magnificent days of its flowering in the medieval schools and of its glory in the Greek academies. In those days it had the sense of unity of the virtuous man whereby everything it did or thought fitted into one organic whole and was thus suffused with light and meaning. But, with its corruption in the Renaissance, with its succumbing to the grave sin of Nominalism, and with its consequent adherence to the false goal of dialectical science it lost these splendors.

The pity is that this need never have occurred. The modern mind need never have opposed itself to the ancient. It need never have lost speculative innocence. Continuity with its past would have enriched it. Then it would have been much happier, as the mind of the virtuous man is happier than the mind of the vicious. But regrettably it did fall into error and has since reaped the consequences from which we are not yet free, although a great step in this direction was taken by the revolt of Kierkegaard. First, we must now see how it came about and then what were its effects.

CHAPTER 9

THE DYNAMISM OF WILL: SIN IN EXISTENTIAL THOUGHT

A sinful life causes spiritual revulsion; since it moves the individual toward a false final term revulsion cannot be avoided. The tension that sin sets up between the false goal and the true goal inevitably causes a nausea that must bring purposeful activity to an end. The spirit, brought thus to a halt, must reverse itself; and instead of ingesting the noxious substance will vomit it out. This is what happened in Kierkegaard's reaction to his religious and cultural milieu. The phenomenon is worth close study.

One of the causes which brought it about was the interconnection between the practical and speculative movements of rational life. Through this interconnection, as we have seen, science comes to be, growing out of practical action and tending toward impractical contemplation. This is why in the Aristotelian tradition virtue is thought to foster contemplation and vice to impede it. Virtue so forms action that it naturally develops into contemplation, and vice so deforms action that contemplation cannot develop.

The importance of this fact cannot be exaggerated. It closely connects theory and contemplation with action, and it is in theory and contemplation that the intellect grows, and as it grows comes more and more to grasp itself in self-consciousness. So action and contemplation facilitate self-consciousness. The growing insights of empirical science do not negate the myth from which they originate, but rather build upon it. They are, to this extent, the flowering of the seeds that myth consciousness plants.

Philosophical consciousness does the same for science. In its highest manifestation in metaphysics, it gives final sense to the investigations of science. To this extent it illuminates scientific induction and theory, and in it the speculative and practical movements of thought are finally united.

When, on the other hand, the spirit through sin and error dissolves its unity, just the contrary is the case, its higher consciousness cannot arise, and its lower consciousness is thus left in darkness. As the error increases the effect intensifies. The final result of this cannot be other than revulsion. This must occur at the moment when, in the spirit, the tension between its chosen false goal and the rejected true one becomes fully known to consciousness. At that moment the spirit by comparing the true and false goals can see their disparity. Through this insight it then realizes the essential impossibility of its chosen goal—that it is an endeavor simultaneously to possess incompatible goods. Seeing this the spirit realizes the futility of its pursuit; and as long as it continues in this fashion, the consequent desperation of its situation. It may be that those who concentrate more on immediate goals and less upon the ultimate do not experience this despair so acutely. But they will still experience it in the lesser intensity of a pervasive sense or feeling of boredom.

Paralleling these two experiences of despair and boredom is a feeling of guilt. Those who feel deep despair feel also profound guilt. On the other hand, those who experience only boredom feel proportionately less guilt. In either case, since it essentially deviates human action from its proper goal sin blocks spiritual development. It does this not by moving a person in the opposite direction to the proper goal, but by making him stop short of it. This stopping short is what causes spiritual nausea.

The intellectual despair of the modern thinker is essentially due to this—he has set for himself a false goal. He has tried to create an empirical science of *being* as such. This is to make empirical science intellectual self-possession—something which it cannot be. The scientist who realizes that this is the contradictory sense of his endeavors necessarily experiences spiritual revulsion.

The revulsion occurs because of nature. It is not the modern thinker's own choice that determines the true end of his speculation. Eventually this is what becomes obvious to him, if only through the experience of spiritual nausea. Through this he comes to see his mind as like a stomach which when it is disposed toward a certain specific comestible regurgitates its opposite.

Kierkegaard's reaction is a witness to this phenomenon. And through his experience he came to realize the truth that the European soul, of which his own was one example, was moving toward a false goal. Later the Existentialists after the devastation of the First World War came to share this conviction. Reeling from the implications of the catastrophe they too came to believe, as Thomas Aquinas had so many years before, that the sinner shatters the unity of his personality.

The modern mind began to move toward this split from its true end when it first chose to make empirical science its ultimate goal. By this choice it made a means into the ultimate end. The first theoretical indication of this tension, to which this inevitably led, was David Hume's critique of Francis Bacon's claim to universality and necessity. Hume argued that science could not achieve certitude by induction. It could, he claimed, achieve no more than subjective expectation.

The thrust of Kant's speculations was to get around the logic of Hume's conclusion. He thought that this could be done by attributing the discovered regularities of nature to the mind as to their cause— empirical science could then maintain its claims. It could use the method of observational induction and still achieve universal insight. Receiving the matter for this from singular sense experience it would impose upon it a priori forms which would assure the universality and necessity of the object. Science could then confidently predict the properties of nature for all time. The objections of Hume would thereby be countered.

But this theory contained its own hidden problems which soon surfaced. As Fichte, Schelling, and Hegel noted it was inconsistent and could be rendered consistent only by further and even more startling suppositions: it had to be supposed that the mind creates not only the form but also the matter of objective experience. In this way, to support the claim that empirical science is ultimate science one had to attribute to it the powers of the creator! This was what Kierkegaard could not do.

Kierkegaard held that man, by reason of his faith stance, is a creature, a dependent being. Therefore as he comes in heightening self-consciousness more and more truly to grasp himself, he must also come more and more profoundly to realize this dependency. And since as he understands himself, he loves himself, it follows that he loves his dependency more intensely. He must therefore find repugnant that urge to think of himself as God; as in effect, the modern empirical mind was urging him to do. In fact Hegel's theoretical justification for it made it so lucidly clear. The religious sense of dependency made it evident to Kierkegaard that Hegel was wrong. This insight then led him to make a critique of the pretensions of the modern mind. The following chapters will present the essence of this critique.

CHAPTER 10

THE ROOTS OF THE KIERKEGAARDIAN REACTION

Kierkegaard on the basis of religious experience rejected Hegel's theory that the Absolute Spirit is the origin and end of both speculation and practice. In his opinion the gratuity of grace makes this impossible. Therefore anyone who attempts to take Hegel's theory seriously, and not only for that specific theory but also for all modern thought insofar as it goes to this, experiences spiritual nausea. Reason of itself alone cannot grasp the ultimate intelligibility of rational consciousness or of the objective world. For Kierkegaard the Divine Mind alone can do this, and the Divine Mind is not in any sense identical with reason! To experience this nausea through an analogue of Kierkegaard's reaction it is necessary to choose a final goal which differs from the one which nature imposes. When we do this, nature, impelling us toward its chosen goal regardless of our choice, brings about revulsion.

It is an impulse of nature that makes empirical science think up dialectical theories and makes philosophy struggle for insight. Both do this in order to move closer to total self-possession. Total self-possession is the true ultimate goal of nature, and nothing short of this will adequately satisfy it. That is why when the mind clearly sees that it is actually moving toward some other goal short of this it experiences nausea. That was Kierkegaard's experience. When he tried to identify himself with God, as Hegel's theory urged him to do, he experienced revulsion. Because of this he totally rejected the Hegelian position.

This was what today we would call an existential rejection rather than a speculative one. From the speculative point of view Kierkegaard could not show where Hegel was wrong. He thought, in fact, that from the speculative point of view that Hegel's theory was probably the best which philosophy could offer. But from the point of view of Christian consciousness, he knew it was wrong—that for the mind it was an indigestible food.

When the stomach tries to digest the indigestible it instinctively reverses its operations and regurgitates. Reversing the normal sequence of muscular contractions, instead of ingesting it expels, and by this rids itself of the content it cannot assimilate. Spiritual regurgitation analogously repeats these phenomena. Such was Kierkegaard's experience by which he reversed the movement of the modern mind. He did this not as a professional philosopher would do it, namely by objective principles and rigorous deduction, but rather as the mystic does—by a mental leap. In view of this, rational justification became for him, if not impossible at least, superfluous.

In this way, Kierkegaard became the first thinker to react existentially against Hegel and, through this, against the self-consciousness of the modern mind. He also rejected Hegel's presuppositions such as the Kantian a priori forms. Since this doctrine led to Hegel it had to be rejected. And for the same reason, so had the claims of positivistic philosophy to be rejected. Positivism through its quasi-scientific methods could not know the truth of being. The rejection of the modern mind was total. Kierkegaard then used this rejection as a dialectical means for reaching the genuine truth of being.

Noting Hegel's claim that reality evolves from Being through the imminent movements of Ego in the dialectic of thesis, antithesis, and synthesis—a claim that made the truth of being logical, and accessible to reason—Kierkegaard could then claim that the truth was, in fact, the opposite. The truth of Being is not rational, but irrational. It is not continuous, but discontinuous. It is contingent and free rather than necessary and forced. For this reason, no one but God knows the intelligibility of Being's inner relations. This is the real truth of Being!

Since the truth of Being is irrational man's metaphysical stance must be that of openness to the absurd, and man's volitional attitude must be that of willingness to accept this. Man must give up any claim to self-sufficiency such as the Hegelian thesis supposes. God alone is the self-sufficient. Man by opening his spirit to God must accept this. He must neither deify the rational nor rationalize the divine. Rather he must accept that the ultimate truth of dependent being is beyond reason and that, whatever his may be, it does not constrain God to make it exist. In act of creating God is completely free. For this reason, the world is thoroughly contingent.

Obviously, Kierkegaard's world differs from the one which positivistic philosophy, basing itself upon Newtonian dynamics, postulates. But the postulate was wrong. The real truth of Being cannot be filtered from nature by observation. Therefore, no empirical law or theory contains it. For this reason, the empirically attainable far from being the real, is just the opposite. The real cannot be measured and is not objective universality.

However, by this conclusion Kierkegaard did not deny in principle that the empirical has any role in the interpretation of Being. Rather, he restricted that role to one of mediation. As long as they are so understood the methods and explanations of empirical science are valid. But when they attempt to go beyond this and truly interpret Being, they are not valid. In this region beyond mediation they simply do not apply. For this reason Kierkegaard hesitates to totally condemn the "system." As long as it confines itself to explaining the intentional structure of the empirical world, he finds it legitimate.

In Kierkegaard's view Hegel's mistake was to have gone further. If he had only seen his theory as an ingenious manifestation of the power of the human mind to construct theories from empirical observations, then he would have shown himself to be perhaps the wisest and the most successful of philosophers. But when he claimed that it unveiled the ultimate structure of being, he became a comic and even a tragic philosopher—a Don Quixote of the discipline, who tried to take an absurd idea seriously.

Hegel's failure does not mean that empirical science is to be totally rejected. With all of its limitations, empirical science is still the means for passing to the true insight. It alone creates the élan which pushes the mind to do this. This is therefore the purpose for which it exists, namely, to provoke the spiritual nausea through which the spirit discovers the ontological and cognitional beyond. Once the spirit knows this it can then strive to possess it. Empirical science in this way leads to the true notion of being. Hegelian philosophy too, to which scientism necessarily gives rise, stimulates the mind to move in the direction of the beyond.

Scientism by creating the hope, and even the conviction, that the scientists will be able to control the world powerfully contributes to this. Captured by the thought that the scientist, by finding the regularities of nature, will make it predictable and thus determine its future, the adherent comes to believe that nature is nothing more than the sum total of those things which scientific techniques can manipulate. He is brought up short when he is confronted with evidence that this is not so—that there are elements of nature which scientific technology cannot control. Nature, he then sees, is partly something beyond technology. This part is uniqueness rather than the universality, subjectivity rather than objectivity. And this part reason cannot manipulate. This is the truth of the matter. Reason is affected—it does not affect. Reason submits—it does not create. This is the essence of the attitude of faith, and because of it the man of faith knows the truth of Being.

In essence, this was Kierkegaard's judgment. He therefore regarded science as means for passing to the ultimate insight itself. The truth of Being, judged from his point of view, has properties diametrically opposed to those which belong to the object of science. It is subjectivity, not objectivity; the unique, not the common; the discontinuous, not the continuous; the irrational, not the rational. To this extent, its properties resemble those of the good which genuine ethics contains. The good of genuine ethics, as contrasted with the good of rational ethics, is not measured by rules and norms, but is unique. And just as the truth of Being it does not deify the human Ego.

Rational ethics, on the contrary, subjects the uniqueness of the individual to common rules. In the last analysis the individual cannot tolerate this, he must then seek out an existential ethics which respects his freedom, and in which, he finds the practical truth of his subjectivity, which is from a rational point of view the absurdity of his true being. This teaches him humility, not presumption, passivity, not domination. These were the qualities Kierkegaard felt predominated in the Christ, the Godman. By his incarnation Christ manifested them perfectly. At once finite and infinite, he was a living contradiction. And he gave us the power to conquer death, not by teaching us rational rules, but by dying for us. Perfection he showed to be found not in carefully observing rational rules, but by blindly trusting in God. Abraham's faith was the pre-figuration of this.

KIERKEGAARDIAN REACTION

A trusting acceptance of contradiction—that was Abraham's faith. On the divine word he believed that he had to sacrifice Isaac, and yet that Isaac would make him the father of a great nation. What he believed was therefore a contradiction, but this did not make him distrust it because his faith itself was essentially irrational. It was an openness to the absurd just as is faith in the incarnation. Such a faith grounds genuine ethics.

Kierkegaard thus bases his teaching upon revulsion for the rational. In the case of Abraham this determines what is genuinely good and what is genuinely true. Kierkegaard can therefore judge in this way the aesthetic, ethical, and speculative evolution of human consciousness. The rational, for him, thus takes its meaning from the revulsion which it causes. Its indispensable role in the development of the soul is precisely this—to cause the revulsion.

Kierkegaard does not therefore reject the rational, rather he delimits its proper role. He makes it a means, not the end. His ironic remarks concerning it are not therefore a call to abandon it but only a demand to place it in its proper context. From this point of view the purpose of his writings was simply to communicate his attitude to others, to make them realize the possibilities of the rational for getting to the truth beyond it and its futility when it is pursued for itself. Hegel it seemed to him fell into a trap—a fundamental error—he saw his system not simply as an ingenious organization by reason of sense experience but as ultimate truth.

In the moral sphere too, Kierkegaard's writings communicate his belief that faith points beyond rational ethics but can only get there by going through it. In the passage through the rational ethics one experiences frustration and even despair, but these are necessary in order for the soul to reach out to the truth beyond.

In short then, Kierkegaard believed that man is put into the world in order that by reason to *attempt* to know the ultimate truth and do the ultimate good. But this is not the ultimate purpose for his creation. The ultimate purpose is that he may, through revulsion for his rational effort, seize the truth beyond and seek its good. This is the true meaning of his existence. Therefore it is a meaning, which finite intelligibility does not exhaust. The soul, knowing this, can give itself to the infinite intelligibility lying beyond. When it does this by free choice it then apprehends the genuine truth of reality—in substance this was Kierkegaard's conviction. In the next chapter, we will consider more of the details.

CHAPTER 11

KIERKEGAARD'S SPECULATIVE THOUGHT

The key to Kierkegaard's thought that the preceding chapters afford can now be used further to unlock the sense of his attitude toward science. This reveals the richness and depth of his reflections.

For Kierkegaard speculative thought has its roots in practical action and knowledge. This primordial knowledge, at least partly abstractive and to that extent unreal, is an initial view of the self and the world. It ties the self to the world through the relation of similarity since it sees the world and the self as sharing common being. This is in fact not true. The self as subjectivity is unique and therefore incommunicable. Therefore a relation which ties it to the world in communality of being destroys it. The primordial practical knowledge which asserts the relation of self and the world does not attain to true knowledge of the self. But it is a beginning, and from it, through spiritual revulsion for it the true knowledge can be reached.

At the beginning of its spiritual growth all this is not evident to the mind. The amount of poison that it consumed in its false consciousness of self is too small to provide a strong reaction. But even this small quantity can provoke some reaction: a dullness of spirit, a mild frustration of hope, a lethargy. To overcome these the mind must, even at the beginning of spiritual growth, view its rational efforts as a means to a contrary insight rather than as a terminal insight in itself. However, the mind does not tend to do this. Rather at the initial stage in its growth it tends to feel that its understanding of nature through reason will give it the power to attain true being and the true understanding of the self. In this attitude, it sees the being of nature as essentially manipulable for human purposes.

By this conception of nature, it stresses nature's community of being with the self and thereby makes the self too simply another thing of nature—like nature capable of manipulation for arbitrary goals. Neither in the case of nature or self is this adequate. Neither can be simple and solely so manipulated. Neither is essentially the abstraction which this view supposes. Rather they are both unique and to this extent share no community of being. The spiritual nausea that we experience when we try to deny this shows that it is so.

The truth is that life is not simply an ordering and a being ordered. It is not simply classification, definition, abstraction, and relation. On the contrary, it is a disordered discontinuity, a contradiction whose true ultimate sense is death. Christ showed us this by dying on the cross.

Naturally enough the rational practical mind denies all of this—it believes that it has the power to take care of itself. It goes unconcernedly about its business in the confident expectation that through growth in knowledge it will actually achieve this power and in the due course of time bring about the reasonable fulfillment of its desires. In Kierkegaard's prognosis it will not do this at all but will only bring about spiritual revulsion by the effort. It will then see that the fulfillment of its hopes does not lie within its power. It will then be seized by despair.

The mind, on the higher level of its social consciousness, will experience a similar result. Its myth insights will be responsible for this. These insights express the communality of social nature and the principles that one must accept to successfully live it. Furthermore, the insights express the meaning of human life that these principles imply. In developing this theme the myth speaks of good and evil, praising the former and condemning the latter. It praises the good which consists in doing those things supportive of the social life. It condemns actions which harm this. To do so is the rational function of the myth. But in its statements concerning good and evil it must not be taken as terminal truth, it is only a mediating level of consciousness necessary to get through to terminal truth. The breakthrough occurs through the Kierkegaardian revulsion, which is what the myth-consciousness eventually precipitates. That myth-consciousness is therefore not simply to be rejected, but rather to be properly used.

Moreover, the myth-consciousness gives rise to the scientific consciousness. Observing things of nature for its own practical purposes it inevitably sees that they follow regular patterns in their operations and passions that are like imminent laws—intentions and purposes written within them that reveal themselves through the laws. Noticing this the myth stimulates the mind to investigate such things for themselves. That is to say, to try to find out what it is that the laws are trying to achieve and through this to learn what they are. In this way science gradually emerges from myth consciousness. When science subsequently leads to the experience of revulsion it simply confirms this experience as it is found in myth-consciousness.

In this way the Kierkegaardian revulsion arises both in myth-consciousness and in scientific-consciousness. Kierkegaard appreciates them both. He does not preach pure and simple rejection of either myth or scientific consciousness but advocates their use for the purpose of breaking through to the ultimate truth. And he pokes fun in his ironies only on those who misuse them by taking them as the absolute term itself.

Thus for Kierkegaard, classification, definition, positing of laws, proposing of theories—all of these rational operations which aim at categorizing reality—are means to an end. They do not directly give the end, but they mediate its acquisition. Thus, the essences and the natures which they uncover are spiritually important. They must therefore be judged as such. Through them alone the mind gets through to the uniqueness of being and of the self. This is the merit of myth-consciousness and of scientific-consciousness. If they are pursued with this in view, they will never harm the spirit.

Positivism errs when it pursues, particularly in the case of scientific consciousness, the rational operations as ends in themselves. It thereby falsely deifies reason. In Kierkegaard's opinion Kant's critique was an endeavor partly to correct this error. It aimed at removing certain logical inconsistencies to which Positivism led, hoping thereby to maintain its substance. In positing a priori forms Kant thought that he had done this. But he had only transferred the communality of the being of nature to the mind. This was a necessary step in the correction of Positivism's exaggerations, but it was a total misconception of the fundamental situation. It failed utterly to realize the subjectivity of being in itself and the uniqueness of the being of things. Thus from the logical point of view it was a success, but from the ontological point of view a failure. Nevertheless, it functioned to reveal the truth. Positing the a priori forms it not only gave a nod in the direction of subjectivity, but also thought far along the path which would make it realize the true situation.

The progress was further heightened by Hegel's speculations. Hegel carried Kant's thought to its logical conclusion. He made the dynamic Ego the first postulate of rationalism. It was his merit to do so and the postulation showed his dialectical genius. But when he thought that he had attained to the meaning of being he made himself ridiculous. By this supposition he made the mind identical with God.

But though this claim was absurd it needed to be made. Through it alone could there come the spiritual revulsion which leads to the truth. This revulsion reveals that the soul is not a dynamic Hegelian Ego and that it is not the creative source of its object of being. The truth of being it shows is irrational, and this fact must be assimilated by the mind through passive openness. Through this it must come to know that the Hegel dialectical triad of thesis, antithesis, and synthesis do not structure being.

All this knowledge is the consequence of Hegel's postulate. This is its real merit. Better than any other body of modern thought it shows the impossible conclusion which follows from overestimating the value of science. In showing this it provides the deepest spiritual purgation.

In essence this is what Kierkegaard had to say: that the pretensions of the modern mind implicit in its attitude toward scientific knowledge are inadmissible. In saying this, he did not make himself simply an iconoclast, nor did he thereby run away from the responsibility of modern thought. Rather, like a mystic he judged it intuitively. In this judgment he saw it as a useful tool rather than the truth in itself.

CHAPTER 12

KIERKEGAARD'S ETHICS AND AESTHETICS

As we have seen Kierkegaard's reaction to the speculative claims of modern thought was critical, although sympathetic. He did not want to destroy it nor belittle its importance. He wanted only to see it for what he thought it properly was, namely a mediating device to strike through to the truth of being. We will now carry these considerations further by studying his reaction to ethics and aesthetics.

I

Kierkegaard could see ethical insight begins, like speculative insight, in the practical. It takes its point of departure in man's awareness of his sensible needs. These are at first purely individual. In seeking their satisfaction man at this stage relates to no one but himself. Operating in this way, he finds that he can satisfy some of these needs easily. But then he begins to discover other needs, in which if he does not cooperate with others, he can satisfy only with great difficulty. Thus when he clearly sees that cooperation is necessary, he develops a social sense. In this way he creates society.

Also in this way he passes from a lower to a high consciousness of his own being. At the lower individual level he thinks of himself as a creature of purely sensible desires, and of his activity as essentially their satisfaction. On the higher social level he thinks of himself as a political animal who must necessarily relate to others, not only to survive but to survive in a pleasing way.

At the social level of consciousness it becomes clear to him that in order to sustain society he must limit his own freedom. If he wishes to sustain society, he cannot do at all times only what he pleases—he must consider the common good. He must have an understanding of the common goals of the community. He must agree with others on the way to achieve the goals. This integral social insight becomes the substance of his myths.

Thus man acquires a social insight and creates the myth—fictitious presentations of value judgments which make those judgments known to the group and facilitate their implementation. In the context of this consciousness man develops customary action. And he judges conformity to that action as good and violation of it as bad. This constitutes his moral consciousness, which in this way is based on custom. Its Latin and Greek names indicate as much. Thus custom symbolically expressed in the myth comes to determine moral consciousness. And society imposes it upon its members for the purpose, not only of survival, but of growth.

For these purposes all myths propose certain similar doctrines. They all deal with the nature of man and with his origin and his future. By relation to him they see the world as rational. They propose a course of action for him in this world and they promise him, if he follows this course, a happy final outcome. They also threaten him with final punishment if he violates its rules. All of this is strikingly expressed in classical Greek drama. In the tragic form of Greek drama it represents human action measured by myth rules. The human actors violate the rules. They then suffer the tragic consequences. In this way the drama presents evil as something to be avoided thereby both inculcating the rules of the myth and urging that they be obeyed.

For Kierkegaard this mythical view of rational life is not the ultimate truth, but a medium for getting to the ultimate truth. For him the myth does not truly tell us what man is, but it gives us a picture which leads to the truth. As a rationalization it abstracts and generalizes, and to this extent, leaves aside the ultimate reality of subjectivity. This is only regained when adherence to myth standards causes spiritual revulsion and through this leads to true insight.

For Kierkegaard the morality of the myth is characterized by its inflexibility. The inflexibility comes from the fact that it gives no evidence to support its claims. Thus being properly poorly understood the claims are not easily modifiable in altered social circumstances. In the *Antigone* Sophocles brings this out well. He will admit of no exception to the careful and reverential burial of the dead. This is a law handed down by the gods, that is to say customary action developed by myth and passed on in traditions. No arguments of reason attempting to show that in particular circumstances it need not be observed have any value against it. When in the Greek drama the protagonists act contrary to custom, they suffer harm. The morality of the rule is inflexible.

Against this sort of morality, in all of its many forms, Kierkegaard launches some of his most bitter attacks. But where Socrates, as portrayed in the Platonic dialogues, attacked it for its lack of insight; Kierkegaard attacked it for its essential fallaciousness. Socrates deplores the following of the myth simply because this is customary and calls for obeying its precepts through insight. Kierkegaard totally rejects the customs, at least as purportedly expressing ultimate moral truth, and preaches rather the essential irrationality of true moral action. He sees blind convention as robbing man of the freedom which this involves. And he sees self-consciously rational virtue as neither the height of human achievement in the moral sphere nor the sense of human life. Above it is free Existential action, and the sense of human life is its irrational openness. Thus in conventional morality he censured precisely the quality through which it appealed to Socrates and Aristotle—its essential reasonableness. Men because of this take it as an absolute norm for conduct, the criterion of the good and the end of existence. But it is really only a mediating phenomenon that by provoking a purgative nausea reveals the true irrationality of being. When this occurs then rational conventional morality is seen for what it truly is: only a valuable aid for spiritual advancement which if it is misused can become dangerous. It tempts the soul to look upon it as an absolute and in so doing keeps the soul from true insight.

Both Christian and pagan forms of conventional morality can be misused and dangerous. In its pagan form, it depends solely upon human social experience. In its Christian form it also depends substantially upon revelation. But in either case if it is not properly grasped it seriously impedes the development of the soul.

The Christian form of conventional morality, it seemed to Kierkegaard, has at least the advantage of being based upon revelation of the irrational, absurd, and contradictory nature of being. In the Incarnation revelation proposed an event at once finite and infinite as its supreme example. In this it achieved the absurd and made the absurd essential to Christian belief. Thus it opened the soul to irrationality rather than closing it off as the pagan myth had done. For this reason the Christian myth must be judged according to an entirely different standard. It is essentially irrational in that it makes death the solution, not the problem.

But if this is so then why did it give rise to a Christian conventional morality? It did so because it failed to make Christians see its essential irrationality. They, blind to the irrationality, fell back upon an essentially pagan conventional morality and sought the same goals: a comfortable life, freedom from poverty and disease, and in personal conduct a reasonable moderation. These goals pervert the Gospel message—the message of happiness through misery, of wealth through poverty, and, as was clear in the crucifixion, of life through death.

In expressing this conviction, Kierkegaard throughout the years of his literary activity, adopted an increasingly bitter tone. Possibly he did this because he felt more and more that he had to shock Christians in order to wean them away from their smug rationality. He did not intend to deny that there is any place for conventional morality in the spiritual growth of a man, but only to assign it its proper place and to determine its mediating function. In this mediating function he considered it to be indispensable for the believer, just as the telescope is indispensable for the astronomer. Once the astronomer has focused on a celestial object, he does not then throw the telescope away. Neither should the believer once he has focused on truth through conventional morality throw it away. Rather, he must preserve, polish, and pursue it—but always as a means to an end not as itself the end.

According to the great pagan conception of classical Greek philosophy conventional morality as virtue was the highest human moral attainment. It was as such action from insight. The insight permitted the one who possessed it to act in particular circumstances with certainty and freedom. It thereby made his operations rational. To do this was for the ancients the essence of virtue. To the pagan notion Kant added the idea of the categorical imperative with its subjective creativity. Hegel then added the further idea, that this and all that the Greek philosophers attributed to virtue, is the imminent expression of itself by Absolute Spirit.

With the Hegelian addition Kierkegaard was convinced the ultimate conceptualization of virtue as rational was reached. As such he was sure it could be only the object of spiritual revulsion through which the spirit would then reach true insight into moral action. It would then see that moral action is ultimately irrational, resting solely upon free choice and openness of spirit. He thought these then are the stages through which man must go in evolving spiritual perfection. The first of these is the stage of the rational. When man has exhausted the possibilities of this he then goes on to the stage of the irrational, and in this finds the ultimate truth.

Kierkegaard's assessment of the morality of his times was harsh. Because it tended to adhere to conventional morality as Christian virtue, he found it totally unacceptable. And he found it all the more distressing in that it was the attitude of Christians, who from the Gospels, should have known better. The Gospels did not teach the contemporary morality of reason and moderation, but another one entirely of contradiction and irrationality. This his fellow churchmen misunderstood completely. Therefore he saw his mission in life to be the correction of this misunderstanding. He was prepared to carry it out even if to do so required him to make such an irritating attack upon them as to call down upon himself their wrath. He felt their irritation itself might shock them into consciousness of their error.

II

Kierkegaard was not alone in his dissatisfaction. Others of his contemporaries too felt the same deep dissatisfaction with the prevailing interpretation of Christian virtue. Therefore, they too did not look to this to find meaning for their lives. They looked instead to the aesthetic rather than to the religious factor to provide meaning. The aesthetic took the place of religion for them and fulfilled many of its functions. Kierkegaard judged this substitution fallacious and of the same sort as the rationality which he found defective in science and ethics.

Their error is evident from the fact that the aesthetic life, to which they turned with such anticipation, has a structure and growth paralleling those of science and ethics. Like science and ethics it too begins in purely practical action. Like both of these too it rises above this practical beginning to achieve its own proper perfection. And it finally realizes this is a totally impractical contemplation of beauty.

Aesthetics is at the beginning similarly outwardly directed. The intelligibility which it sees at that stage is that of the tool that is ordered to something outside of itself, whose intelligibility is this external relation to the work to be accomplished. But art as it develops, turns this relation into the art object itself and thereby gives it an intrinsic and imminent intelligibility which has no outside reference. In this way it separates out the independent intelligibility and value of the art object, thus making it no longer a means to an end, but an end in itself—an object purely and simply for contemplation. In this way, just as science and ethics, art passes from the practical to the useless, from the practical to the contemplative. In the end, like science and ethics, it becomes purely impractical. Where science becomes impractical, philosophy and ethics become self-validating action, art becomes that which when seen purely and simply pleases.

Therefore, the term in each case of science, philosophy, ethics, and art, is inward directedness. From an original reference to what is without they each reach a final reference to itself—a full interiority. This is the essential truth. It reveals that in all of its activity, without exception, the mind is really seeking itself. And, when it critically discovers this then it discovers the terminal interiority of the scientific, the ethical, and the aesthetic.

The mind discovers this in each case through the Existential experience. How this happens in science where the search for rational essences leads to speculative nausea and thus reveals the genuine truth of being, we have already seen. We also have seen how it happens in ethics where the original pursuit of purely rational norms and rules leads to moral revulsion and, through this, to knowledge of the genuine good. Now we must consider how this process occurs in art. Because art parallels the scientific and the aesthetic in its growth, we may confidently expect that the procedure will be the same, and therefore that it will produce aesthetic revulsion from which true insight into beauty then results.

This is, in fact, what happens. In the realm of art the soul is at first immersed in practicality. It makes tools and other such things for their utility, that is to say for their relationship to an extrinsic thing whose production they facilitate. But at a certain time it begins to see other than external relations in the tool. At this time, it experiences the aesthetic.

How it does this is easily surmised. Suppose that the tool in question is a knife. The maker sees that this is more adapted to its end if its shape is symmetrical. Then it balances better in the hand and is more easily used. But at the same time it then has the intelligibility of the *internal* relationship of symmetry. This ties together the parts of the knife it does not relate it to anything external. Thus it is an imminent intelligibility. The mind, recognizing this appreciates the aesthetic. For this is what essentially the aesthetic is—the imminent intelligibility of the work of art.

In this way in art the mind discovers the impractical in the practical, and through externally connecting relations internally connecting ones. In this discovery the mind applies, as it were, a filter to the practical object that takes out the external relations and leaves only the internal ones. This residue is the purity of the aesthetic. The mind viewing it as such finds pleasure in this. It thus becomes conscious of that which when seen pleases. By this consciousness it passes over the borderline between the practical and the aesthetic. A new world and new possibilities of experience thus open up for it.

This new world ranges all the way from a lower level where it just clears the practical to the highest possible where it is completely free of any element of practicality. Throughout this range it is continuous passing at each step without a break into the next. Thus, imperceptibly its lowest practicality becomes its highest impracticality, and its lower utility becomes it higher uselessness. Such is its nature.

As a result of this process at its highest point the aesthetic world parallels in abstraction and universality the worlds of science and ethics. At this level eliminating, as science and ethics do, all relation to the extrinsic thing to be made and taking on the quality of the contemplative—of that which is simply to be seen, possessed through this, and enjoyed. Thus where the scientific becomes thoroughly useless in metaphysics, and the ethical in highest rational virtue, the aesthetic becomes useless in contemplating a work of art. For in such a contemplation it is no longer a medium for obtaining a good, but it is that good itself.

The aesthetic nausea is provoked, in the course of this activity, by a rationalism of making that endeavors to establish rational beauty as the true ultimate one. By the revulsion that then occurs the mind knows that this is wrong. It knows, at the same time, that the greatest mistake it can make is to identify the mediating activity which is the pursuit of rational beauty as an ultimate, with that ultimate in itself. This is the mistake which stunts the soul.

For Kierkegaard this is the mistake which the rationally aesthetic man makes. He falsely judges that the rationality of his aesthetic efforts is true and ultimate beauty. To achieve the ultimate he must give up his false notion and see rational aesthetics for what it really is—mediating aesthetics. Through it he can break the barrier which separates him from infinite beauty. This true beauty is unique. It is the subjectivity of being and not the objectivity of the tool. Aesthetic nausea shows this to be true. In the development of his aesthetic insight it is, therefore, not only permissible, but mandatory that the artist should allow this to take place. If he does not, he will never know the real truth.

These are the three movements of the rational spirit in the thought of Kierkegaard, and they all have the same common end—the possession of the true self. Kant, and above all Hegel for whom the Ego was not only the term but also the beginning, made this clear. They showed that from the unity of the Ego the three movements branch out, and to the unity of the Ego they return. Kierkegaard added the qualification that the return involves a nausea experience. Through this addition he reinterpreted Hegel. The truth of being he then determined is not rational, but irrational; its goodness is not logically consistent, but absurd; and its beauty is not consistent, but chaotic. This does not mean that the mind, in seeking it can bypass the rational and directly intuit the higher truth. This it cannot do. In terms of this we can interpret its every stage. In the next chapter, this will be our concern.

CHAPTER 13

THE KIERKEGAARDIAN MEANING OF LIFE

Human life begins by creation that places man into the world. Within the framework of the world man then develops rational activity. Through the experience of nausea for this rational activity man then finally contacts absolute truth, goodness, and beauty. Such is the Kierkegaardian picture of life!

Therefore, a life is successful if it gets past the intermediate rational stage and penetrates into the truth of being. If it fails to do so then it is unsuccessful and bogs down indefinitely in the intermediate stage making the rational its measure. This indefinite meandering in the intermediate is the essence of its failure.

The successful life attains the true goal of the truth of being by breaking through to this by using its rational activity as a medium rather than an end. It thus correctly interprets the meaning of the rational and derives all the good which it possibly can from this. It may not do this at the very beginning, but when it does, it will then reflect back upon the path which it has followed and truly understand it.

This was God's purpose in creation as indefinitely many texts of sacred scripture show. His creative intention they say is irrational, contradictory, and incomprehensible. This is the truth and God calls upon us to recognize it, to open our souls to its infinity and not to close them up in the false notion of the finite rational world. This is in fact, the substance of revelation.

To communicate it perfectly to us in words he sent Christ, his Son into the world to manifest it in the flesh—that is to say to embody its concrete irrationality. Christ does this by being both God and man—at once finite and infinite. He does this also through his actions, chiefly through his irrational quest for life in death. His cross was his supreme folly. The Greek philosophers who heard Saint Paul were of this opinion, but they were wrong in thinking that the irrationality should have therefore been rejected. It should rather have been embraced as the embodiment of the truth of being. This was the acknowledgement for which God made them, He made them for the purpose of rising to the consciousness of the absurdity of being. The man who achieves the insight is successful, the one who does not is a failure. So Kierkegaard thought.

From this Kierkegaard concluded that the act of irrational acceptance is the greatest of all. As with the act of faith of our father Abraham, it demands humility and obedience of will and openness of intellect. Through these it merits before the Creator and makes us worthy of his praise.

Deprived of these qualities of the soul we are not worthy of God's praise. We have, so to speak, disappointed him and merited his condemnation. We have failed to adhere to him and have chosen to adhere to the rational as the truth of being, something much less than the ultimate truth of being. In doing this we have made God rational, that is to say we have fashioned him in our own image and likeness—reversing the biblical order of dependence. In this we have committed the sin of idolatry, and therefore it is not surprising that in the speculative, ethical, and aesthetic fields we should identify ourselves with God. If we can fashion God to our own image and likeness, why can we not deify ourselves?

We might understand this perverted action as the breaking of a moral rule. But we may also understand it as putting our spirits into prisons from which we cannot then escape. This second understanding of the sin is the more profound and the one closer to the essential truth. It does not, as does the first, measure the sinful act by a rational standard. And it takes into account the quality of transcendence in sin, namely that sin rises above all finite limitations even if committed in finite circumstances of time and place. It is, in essence, a qualitatively infinite act.

Some of the more recent Existential authors seem not to understand the quality of transcendence in sin sufficiently well, if at all. Thus they present rational-sin *qua* sin as the adequate medium for the insight into true moral being, whereas Kierkegaard holds that it is rational-sin *qua* rational which is really this. He thereby makes rational activity as such—rather than conditioned rational sinful activity—the medium for the Existential nausea. With this position he implies that the good rational action, the virtuous action, is also, and even more so, the mediating principle. This is because it embodies rationality even more perfectly than does rational sin. Therefore it provokes a stronger reaction.

Some of the writers on Existentialism seem not to grasp this aspect of Kierkegaardian thought and so they confuse rational sin with Existential insight. They seem to reason that since both are diametrically opposed to rational virtue, they are on that account the same. Therefore these writers hold true moral insight is to be sought through sin. This opinion, which has no theoretical justification, has wide-spread influence even outside of secularist circles. But the strongest possible theoretical considerations are against it. In the light of these considerations it must be held that the medium for the purgative insight is not primarily sinfulness, but rationality.

In more recent times the failure to see this has given rise to the so-called "Situation Ethics." Basing their position on Kierkegaard's conception of the essence of man as uniqueness they hold that this follows also for his actions, therefore these actions cannot be reduced to rules—effectively eliminating moral principles, or at least seriously curtailing their range of application. Rules as universal and common entities they cannot touch the unique individuality of man, therefore they do not say the last word on his concrete actions. These actions then may operate by "rules" which change for each circumstance. This is the same as to say that there are really no such rules at all. So say the "Situation Moralists," but they base this statement upon a misunderstanding of Kierkegaard.

Kierkegaard did not hold that it is the quality of sinfulness in the sinful action which opposes it to truth. Rather, he held that it is the quality of rationality that is found most perfectly in virtuous action, and which as manifesting itself there as applied principle, opposes it to truth. Far from rejecting moral principles by this he supported them. Only by applying moral principles, that is to say by considering human action as amenable to such principles, can one create, for him, the conditions in which the Existential nausea can occur. In this opinion he hardly provides a base of Situation Ethics.

Nevertheless, he does admit of an accidental sense in which sin as such may play an important role. In that it strips away rational hopes and leaves behind despair, it mirrors something of the genuine quality of itself, less eager to try to control the world by its own resources and therefore more open to the irrational. For this reason, the Christian tradition has always praised the recognition of one's sinfulness before God as an attitude conducive to sanctity. This has never meant that the Church has recommended sin in order to achieve this attitude.

Therefore, the essential truth of the matter is not that we must sin in order to have access to God, or that at least this is the best way to do so, but rather that we must pursue the rational to the point of nausea. This is not the same thing as pursuing the life of sin. Nevertheless, if we fail by pursuing a sinful life, we can still through it, as rational, achieve true insight into being and morality. It is a lesser medium for this but a possible one.

Judged in the light of this, man's real defection is not from a rational standard which he fails to apply properly, but from a lack of openness to the infusion of the divine irrationality. By sealing himself into the rational he closes himself off. Feeling himself sufficient there he excludes God. This is what Hegel explicitly did, and it was what scientific thought throughout the modern period implicitly did. It was man's true sin.

The truth is the contrary of the conclusion that rationality is sufficient, and sin is abhorrent to the God of truth. This is why, to correct the state of affairs he directly revealed to man the irrationality of the situation, in so many words, he told man that reason cannot comprehend God's work. God made clear the world is free, not necessary. Only by faith in this word does man achieve the truth.

Being convinced that this is the truth of the matter Kierkegaard wanted, by the pen, to impress it deeply into the minds of his contemporaries. He felt that if he did not do this the message would decay, as apparently it already had done. To counteract this he felt someone has always to present it anew. There must always be the new preacher!

KIERKEGAARDIAN MEANING OF LIFE

Kierkegaard chose the form of irony for his presentation of the message. He scolded and chided his readers and the institutions of society. He did this not as an iconoclast, but as a restorer, a re-animator, and a renovator. He was a prophet pleading the case of an ancient wisdom. While he may have been a voice "crying in the wilderness," he was not thereby a fanatic. He was rather a preacher in the tradition of the great prophets.

The message that he preached, not as something entirely new nor as his own discovery but as something very old of great worth, was the message of the true meaning of life. For different men in different conditions this has many meanings. But only one is true—the meaning of the act of faith. Such was God's message to man. Kierkegaard's intention was to heighten it by literary presentation and thus to impress it deeply in the minds of his contemporaries. He felt this was necessary to keep it from becoming stale. To enliven the message the preacher must always present it under a new and stimulating form.

For different men, according as they tend to different ultimate goals, life has different meanings; but only one of these is true. Others of a rational character, insofar as they set honor, or power, or fame, or wealth, or any other intermediate as the ultimate end; they are false. The ultimate end of life is irrational. This was Kierkegaard's message!

According to the rational picture which Christians all too often accept, life began with a rational creation. God brought being out of nothingness as a craftsman shapes a tool out of metal. He separated the dry land from the waters for the reasonable purpose of preparing dwelling places for the land and sea animals. He then mixed the land and the sea to form slime and breathing on the slime gave it life. In this way, the rational belief would have it, he created living things and ultimately man. He did this again for the reasonable purpose of manifesting his own glory. Such was, for the rational myth, the creation of the world. But is this myth true? Did things come into being in this way? Can reason truly understand their origin? Does reason attain to existence and explain it? These are the serious questions which the rational myth poses.

At first glance, it might appear that these questions are to be answered in the affirmative, for the creation story is presented to us as God's word. He affirms its truth, or at least seems to do so. And he cannot deceive. Therefore the biblical creation myth must, it would seem, be the truth of the matter.

But on the other hand this is impossible. The truth of being is not rational, but irrational! For this reason, being cannot have a rational beginning and ending. At all times it must remain essentially absurd. But essences, since they are products of the abstracting rational mind, cannot be absurd. Only existence, since it is the opposite of essence, can be absurd. The mistake of the rational approach to creation is not to recognize this. Thus it becomes abstractive. Existence clearly is not abstractive. It is unique. It is an act which takes place once and for all, which is not, for this reason, really in time and space, and therefore is not repeated. To conceive of it as if this were not so is to falsify existence.

If this is true, then what does Divine revelation mean? In affirming the myth of a rational creation, such as God does in the revealed books, does he lie? Clearly, he does not, insofar as he indicates time and time again in the sacred writings that the picture is not ultimate truth. He clearly corrects any false impression which it might give. Repeatedly stressing the contingency and liberty of his creative act, he affirms that it operates upon no matter. Time and time again, he says that he was without constraint in producing the world, and that in his dealings with it he is completely free. "I will show mercy upon whom I will show mercy," He says, and "upon whom I will not show mercy, I will not show mercy." This is the declaration of one who is completely free and who is forced by no rational necessity. He could just as well have done the contrary. To the extent that this is true it is clear that for his choice there is no rational explanation. If there were a rational explanation it would thereby destroy the freedom of the act—God time and time again in his revelation makes this clear. Therefore in so doing he does not deceive us.

In the opening book of the Bible, he tells us that he looked upon the world, and finding it good was pleased with it like an artist pleased with his work. But he does not affirm that desire for this pleasure forced him to create the world. Quite on the contrary, he makes clear that, by creating it, he gains no advantage. Only because he freely chose to do so did he breathe upon the chaos. This free choice is thus the ultimate explanation of the world.

He makes this freedom even clearer in his insistence that his creative act had no matter upon which to work. He brought the world into being out of nothing. It emerged therefore from that which *was not,* and it thus always bears upon itself the stamp of this nothingness. But this means that from the viewpoint of rational thought it is negation. It means that the emergence of the world from nonbeing is its emergence from irrationality. The world is thus the child of the irrational, and it must therefore resemble its parent. In revealing this God does not deceive us concerning the truth of things.

Thus the true picture of the world which God reveals is the contrary of the rational myth, and the Existential nausea is simply another way of knowing this. It too teaches us that we cannot adhere to the rational as to an absolute and that, for this reason, we must view the contrary, the irrational, as our true mental food. It teaches us neither the creation nor the conservation of being is rational and from a rational point of view it cannot be given an ultimate explanation.

The ultimate explanation of being is that it is irrational and unique both in its beginning and in its continued existence. Therefore neither temporally nor in any other way can it be divided into parts. It is thoroughly simple. It does not emerge in time and develop toward a rational goal. A material goal for it is fictitious—it is inauthentic being. In his rational existence man has this inauthentic being. This existence has no independent value in itself. It has value only as a means to that which is genuine.

Nevertheless rational existence is important—one must not underestimate it. Only through it can man reach genuine being. Only through rational existence, with its abstracting, relating, and classifying, is this possible for him. He cannot penetrate to genuine being directly. He must have a rational history first. This is his only door.

The truth, which he thus achieves *through* rational existence is quite different from rational truth. It is a genuine understanding of his own uniqueness. The truth is he has no beginning in time and space. All he has is an opening of his soul to the absurd, by which he makes contact with genuine being. Through this opening, he communes with being rather than through the rational connection of cause and effect. How different this "truth being" is from the inauthentic being. By it, man does not come to be in time. By it he does not begin to exist at a definite moment in the history of the rational world. This is true being!

By false being, man develops within a material framework, growing toward a rational goal which he can comprehend and which he can thus relate to other similarly finitely comprehensible things. Thus he progresses in science, virtue, and art. The progress, since it is complex, is therefore inauthentic being. By adding part to part, perfection to imperfection, it divides and thus falsifies simple existence. It cannot be a genuine mode of true existence, but only a fictitious one whose sole purpose is to mediate.

Only by increasing the intensity of his possession of simple existence can man possess true being. This is the truth of the matter and man must learn to live by it! That is to say he must interpret his rational existence as a means to his ultimate beingness. He must interpret his rational history as a means for attaining authentic being. This is his sole function.

When man misuses his rational history, as all too often he does, he places an obstacle in the way of spiritual growth. This distracts his mind from its true purpose and occupies it indefinitely with an insoluble problem rather than an easy passage to authentic existence. For if the former is a medium for the latter then when the intensity of its rationality mounts so also must its mediating potentiality.

Man according to the rational interpretation of human history was put into a good world by God in order that man might relate rationally to him, please him, and by this, thus merit eternal happiness. But by introducing sin into the world man disturbed its order and thereby displeased God. This sin was man's failure to observe God's reasonable command that man avoid eating the fruit of a certain tree in the Garden of Eden. As a rational rule this was abstract and universal. It was a measure of good and evil. Man by eating the forbidden fruit did evil. In this way he introduced sin into the world. This sin at its heart was one of pride. In committing it man chose himself rather than God as his norm and thus denied his dependency. God therefore drove him out of the Garden of Eden and forced him to gain his happiness.

From Kierkegaard's point of view man by his sin deified the rational making it the ultimate truth, and himself therefore the ultimate being. This in substance is what he always does when he sins. He thus shuts himself off from God by closing the only avenue of his soul through which he could contact God. Sealing over this opening he locks himself within. This is what he did in originally introducing sin into the world, and this is what he does whenever he again commits sin. Hegel, in his doctrine of the dynamic Ego made this formally evident. And unless God forces his way past the barricade and makes man conscious of the truth it dooms man to eternal frustration in the pursuit of a false goal, and thus to inauthentic living.

Because of what the Christian myth rationally presents as his pity for men this is what God decided to do. Seeing the misery of their inauthentic mode of existence he took pity upon men and determined to help them. To do this he first revealed to them the truth of their situation—that they were living inauthentic lives; that rational insight could not explain the fact of their existence. He revealed this by praising those who obeyed his irrational commands. This Abraham did when he undertook at God's order the sacrifice of Isaac while believing that through Isaac he would father a great people. God revealed this by censuring Pharaoh for not freeing his people, but at the same time making it clear that he could, if he so chose, convert Pharaoh. As he himself put this "irrational" way of dealing with men: "I will have mercy on whom I will have mercy, and upon whom I will not have mercy, I will not have mercy!" By these and many other indications, he made clear to men that the truth of being is irrational and that their refusal to accept this is the root of their misery.

God went much further, and in the irrational Incarnation of his Son most profoundly manifested the irrational in the flesh. For Christ, the finite-infinite, the man-God, was the absurd in the flesh. Seeing him men saw the concretized irrationality of being. This was why he came. This was his mission.

Christ was concretized irrationality not only in his being but also in his actions. His actions showed that for him the norm of moral goodness is not rational rules, but the irrational uniqueness of the moral situation. Thus, by dying he sought life, and by embracing poverty he sought to possess the world. To the rational Greek for whom death was the problem—not the answer—this made him unintelligible. When Saint Paul preached Christ crucified the rational Greek refused to take Saint Paul seriously.

By the folly of his crucifixion Christ mediates moral and speculative truth. From the rational point of view this passion was a tragedy, a defeat. But from an irrational point of view it was a success. It pointed beyond itself to the irrationality of the free creative act through which being exists. It made manifest the truth that this irrationality is the substance of being a substance which faith alone apprehends—faith which is supreme trust in the unknown. In adhering to the person of Christ and to his teaching, the mind must give this faith to him.

For Kierkegaard the most abhorrent interpretation of the life of Christ was the rational one. This he thought to be the interpretation of his contemporary Protestant brothers, for whom as Kierkegaard said, God was a supreme benefactor making up for gaps in nature that prevented rational goals from being achieved. God was the one to whom a person prayed for success in business and to whom a person expressed gratitude when he achieved success. God was a remedy for deficiencies and religiosity was prosperity. Kierkegaard felt this was totally against the sense of the gospel message. Christ did not represent security, but rather insecurity. Christ did not represent understandable presence of God, but his mystery. The gospel message was, in short, not the bourgeois God of the Protestants. So thought Kierkegaard.

As a consequence Kierkegaard felt the true God does not fulfill rational expectations. That is why God permitted Christ, contrary to Christ's express prayer, to die on the cross. That prayer was the embodiment of every rational prayer that is ever uttered to God, and by answering it God would most perfectly have exemplified himself as a rational God. But he did not do so. He rejected it and manifested himself rather as an irrational God. He went against the wishes of Christ for his greater good—namely glorification. He acts in the same way with every Christian who understands the message, and, in its genuine spirit, adheres to it, and with every Christian who patterns his life, not after the rational ethics of the pagans, but after the irrational ethics of Christ.

In this respect the history of the human race, not only morally but also scientifically and aesthetically, has been one of failure. In all of these fields, humanity has advanced in rational understanding but not in penetration to the real truth of being. And this failure has, over the years, become greater. To Kierkegaard it seemed that in his time it had become extreme.

Hegel had brought rational insight into the meaning of life to its absolute height by specifically identifying the ultimate goals of the speculative and the ethical in his theory of the dynamic Ego. This insight the mind could not possibly accept. The merit of Hegel's thought had been, by identifying it with clarity, to show that this was so. The Ego, thus exposed, had been in fact the source of the modern malaise. For the mind cannot even partly accept it without some sort of incipient revulsion, even though this may remain relatively mild. This was the root of the dissatisfaction and uneasiness which had been so characteristic of modern times. It is a malaise which reason can provoke in the mind, but which it cannot cure.

For the soul caught in this distressing situation only two reactions are possible. The one is to regress to the lower rational levels where the discomfort is less intense; the other is to face the discomfort in all its intensity directly and provoke the nausea. The first escape is not a true one because it only temporizes with the problem; inevitably it leads the soul back again into the same disquieting situation. With courage it can hope through the direct confrontation to break out into the true world of the irrationality of genuine being.

In the light of this, Kierkegaard's message for his times was that men should courageously avail themselves of the means to penetrate the truth of being. This is their true vocation. This is why, in the final analysis, God put them in the world. This is the irrational reason for their existence.

CHAPTER 14

VARIETIES OF EXISTENTIAL DOCTRINE

Kierkegaard's interpretation of the meaning of being through the medium of Existential revulsion is not unique. There are many forms other than his which it can take. In all of them the subjective conditions of the particular thinker are crucial—the variety of Existentialist philosophies which have developed in the past half century make this evident. But they all have, in spite of their differences, a connection with Kierkegaard's original thought.

I

Phenomenology mediates this. Without Phenomenology, the contemporary Existentialist philosophies could not have arisen—at least not in their present form. A peculiar difficulty in Kierkegaard's thought with which Phenomenology comes to grips would have made this impossible. For although Kierkegaard preaches irrationality, he preaches it in rational terms. To that extent his doctrine is inconsistent.

His doctrine denies that the truth of being is rational, but in this statement it employs the terms "truth" and "rational" and "being." But these terms are themselves rational and are from a rational context. Therefore these terms would seem not to be available to express an irrational content—except perhaps through negation. To be used in this context they must first be purged of the specifically rational meaning. The technique for accomplishing this is Phenomenology.

It must be applied not only to speculative words such as those given but also to practical words. Ethics uses rational words dealing as it does with the "good" and with "obligation." But both are, again according to Kierkegaard, irrational. The "true" and "good" is not for the Danish philosopher the correspondence of action to rational goals but precisely the opposite of this. Is this peculiar use of both terms consistent? Clearly it is not. One way for escaping the Kierkegaardian dilemma is to consider such terms as strictly confined to the rational, but symbolically mediating the irrational through negation. Another way to accomplish the same goal is to take the Phenomenological way out.

Phenomenology begins by distinguishing things as they are in themselves from things as they are in thought. This is a traditional scholastic distinction with a long history in philosophy. Phenomenology uses it to stipulate that its concern is things as they are in thought. For such things it is concerned with essences, that is to say, with what pertains to them essentially and not contingently.

This is not a psychological concern such as it would be, for example, if Phenomenology were interested in the temporal sequence of notions in a particular mind or in many particular minds. This is not its interest at all. It therefore abstracts from the subjective self. It tries rather to discover the stable objective structure of ideas. It wants to know what essentially pertains to them in their objectivity. The motivation behind this seems similar to that behind semantics, in that whereas semantics takes words themselves as the causes of mental problems, Phenomenology takes concepts as this cause. And like semantics it denies that the cause is real.

For existentialists trying to take up where Kierkegaard left off this method is especially apt. In distinguishing between the thing in itself and the thing as conceived it permits them to take rational ideas, such as "truth" and "good" and "being," and purge them of their specifically rational content without totally depriving them of meaning. Having done this, they can then justify Kierkegaard's expression of his irrational thought in rational terminology. This overcomes the difficulty of inner inconsistency. Existentialism thus establishes its right to express and communicate itself in common language.

Beyond a certain unity in methodology given to it by Phenomenology and a certain general manifestation of similarity of

VARIETIES OF EXISTENTIAL DOCTRINE

structure due to its common method of origin (the nauseating spiritual experience), the doctrine which then expresses itself has an enormous diversity. The diversity is so great that some of those who adhere to particular variants of the doctrine will not accept the common name. They do not wish to be called Existentialists. Some, for example, see themselves as more concerned with being rather than with existence. Others do not want the name since it signifies an abstract doctrine.

II

The roots of the Existential diversity lie in the indefiniteness of the nausea principle. According to this principle as Kierkegaard interpreted it, the mind though its revulsion for a particular mental diet learns what its true food is. And through its revulsion for rational morality it learns that irrational morality is a genuine good. And through its revulsion for rational science it learns that its basic desire is irrational intuition.

In every such case, in which the truth is discovered revulsion is the means. But as a means it is indefinite, for it really only tells us that the truth is contrary to what we think it to be. It does not tell us specifically what this contrary is. Just as physical nausea does not tell us specifically what we should eat, so spiritual nausea does not tell us specifically what we should think and do. Therefore upon our own initiative we must make a choice. The diversity of the motives behind this choice diversifies Existentialist doctrines. While this is at least in part true, there is also another cause.

The second cause responsible for the variety of Existentialist thought is the diversity of the diets which trigger off the nausea reaction. This is the more immediate cause of the diversity and it is widely recognized as such—Philosophers experience the nausea for different spiritual diets. Their Existentialist thought reflects this. In that way, they are diversified.

Existentialist doctrines arising as they do from different experiences have, to this extent, no common specific content. In that they are therefore thoroughly subjective they have, as a consequence, the incommunicability which is the essence of subjectivity. Many Existentialists have for this reason chosen the aesthetic to express their thought, for this alone seems capable of it. The result has sometimes been tedious to the point of tears—which may perhaps have been intentional—but as communication of the experience it has not always been successful.

In any event, the diversity of the doctrine is due to the stated two causes and can in every case be traced back to them. Due to the obvious complexity of the first cause, it would not be practical for us to engage here in a study of it. But we may profitably pass a few moments in the study of the relatively simple diversity-of-spiritual-diets cause.

III

Let us do this first of all in the case of Heidegger. Up to the moment of nausea this philosopher goes along with Kierkegaard. On the basis of personal experience, he admits the existence of this nausea. And, as a means for attaining the true diet of the mind, he admits its value. But from this point on he goes his own way. Where Kierkegaard rejects metaphysics as a means for gaining a true insight into being, Heidegger embraces it.

The Existential nausea, he observes, reveals to the soul the true nature of being thus making it aware of the fact that the rational notion is entirely false. Where previously the soul had looked upon being as the apex of the rational it now rejects this. The experience of nausea shows it that its own spirit is violently antipathetic to this belief. The soul now knows being is not the supreme rational genus, but something beyond this. The prime problem of thought is therefore that of the nature of being, and the prime mistake of thought is to misconceive this.

Heidegger does not see himself as seeking existence as opposed to essence, but as seeking the meaning of being. For this reason, he does not want to be called an Existentialist. For him Existence is not the

VARIETIES OF EXISTENTIAL DOCTRINE

essence of being, but only a means to it. This alone is what philosophy must pursue. Therefore he takes being as the goal of his investigations. They are for the purpose of baring the meaning of being purged of its rational content and revealed for what it is in itself.

This purpose obviously makes him more like the ancient metaphysicians than the literary Kierkegaard. But it also makes him depend essentially upon methodology for justification. Without this latter he would seem to fall into the impossible position of rising above the rational by a discussion which is itself essentially on the rational level. Using technique he attempts to avoid this by purifying the traditional concepts. With this purged matter he is able to construct an ontology which is similar to the ancient in its intentional structure but totally different from it in its content. At least this is what he presumes to do.

Thus, in Heidegger's chief work, *Sein und Zeit*, he approaches the task of finding the true meaning of being. He affirms, the central problem of all thought is the true meaning of being, but that it is a problem that has been unfortunately neglected in more recent times. In what may seem a surprising concession, he goes on to say, the true meaning of being received from Aristotle is the most profound contribution—even though not a completely successful one. This was the doctrine of the analogy of being.

In discussing it Aristotle pointed out, as does Existentialism itself, that being is not a genus—a common universal category which by restriction through specific differences descends to particulars. Transcending genera and involving them all in itself through this transcendence, he said it is in them all and identical to none of them. In order that it be such, it must necessarily have not an absolute content, but an analogous or proportional one. It must therefore be essentially relative.

Behind this doctrine of the Stagirite was a profound argument. He reveals that only three affirmations can be made of being:

1. that it is a univocal content of thought,
2. that it is equivocal,
3. that it is analogous.

The argument held that it was evident the first could not be the case. This position as proposed in the profound speculations of the Eleatics, affirmed that being is an absolute content found in all things, as a genus is in its species. This seems the most natural opinion, but it concludes that the multiplicity of things is illusion. This follows from the consideration that, if the supreme genus of being is to be found in many particular beings, this must be because their distinction lies outside of it. But outside of it there is only non-being. This is to say that nothing distinguishes them, or that they are not distinct at all. They are one. Being is not multiplied. To Aristotle since this was a necessary and an absurd conclusion of the opinion that being is a genus, he therefore rejected it.

No other serious thinker who argued with Aristotle tried to counter the Eleatic conclusion by holding that being is equivocal. (One might, however, argue that this was substantially the position of the Sophists.) All clearly saw that to hold this was to make any affirmation concerning being impossible. Such a position would be negating, that is, self-destroying. But no other one of them proposed specific alternatives.

In this way, as in many other doctrines, Aristotle showed the uniqueness of his genius. He reasoned that, if we cannot maintain that things are absolutely diverse and in no way one, because this makes the concept of being equivocal and unintelligible, nor that they are absolutely one and in no way diverse, since this makes being univocal and concludes that there is only one being, we must therefore maintain that beings are absolutely diverse and only in some way one. This is the third and only remaining possibility. It makes the concept of being neither univocal nor equivocal, but in between, closer to the equivocal extreme. It is therefore not one absolute content which things share as a common genus. Rather, it is a relational one. As such, it has properties contrary to those of a genus such as, for example, that it can actually contain its differences within itself.

To Heidegger, at the time of the composition of his most famous work, this profound theory seemed to be in all of philosophy the greatest contribution to the understanding of being. But, nevertheless, he did not think that it was a complete solution. In it

VARIETIES OF EXISTENTIAL DOCTRINE

lay too much of the rationalism which the existential nausea reveals to be not true insight into being.

But what is the content of this true insight? In the spirit of Heidegger, we must be careful first of all, not to conceive of it as we conceive of the content of objective rational thought. And we may speak of it in what were originally rational terms only because we have first phenomenologically purged them. On the other hand, since its content is that of transcended rationality, it always involves the rational as its point of origin, and this means the immersion of the self in particular rational situations above which the self then rises through nausea, through which it sees the truth of being. This content is therefore one in its transcendence and multiple in its situation-rooted origin. To discover this variety, one must therefore investigate the richness of its origin.

In this respect, it is important to remark that Heidegger, different from Kierkegaard, does not think that God must necessarily emerge in the context of the existential nausea and the subsequent transcendence of the rational. Within this context, the self alone must emerge. It alone must transcend, and it alone is sufficiently being. It needs no extrinsic reference to support this sufficiency. For the self, in Heidegger's thought, the notion of God is thus dispensable.

If achieving a true insight into being is a transcending by which the self rises above its rational situation, as Heidegger theorizes, then it is a coming to possess true self, which is to say, at least one true being. And if achieving an insight into being in general is going beyond this then it is a secondary transcendence in which the self rises above its own particularity. Thus it is a process from insight to nausea, to true insight into the being of the self, to true insight, by transcendence of the particularity of self, into the being of Being. With this final insight it makes its term.

In Heidegger's *Sein und Zeit*, the program was to document these steps of possessing the true self and transcending that. They therefore are its divisions, and in it, somewhat as Hegel did in the Phenomenology, he intends to reveal exactly how they unfold. Though the fact is, that though he was unable to carry this program through, it is, despite the demurrers, to his admirers an eloquent commentary on its plausibility. Heidegger was able to achieve in fact no more of the program than the phenomenological description of the human mode of being. This failure does not concern us here. What does concern us of Heidegger's program is the mature variant of Existentialism insofar as it manifests the general nature of all Existential thought.

Heidegger's Existentialism, as all other Existentialisms, brings with it a spiritual reaction to the rational content which the culture of the modern era attempts to feed into the modern mind. This reaction makes him one with Kierkegaard. But from this original agreement he takes a different direction. Where Kierkegaard eschews the rational Heidegger introduces it liberally into his thought. He thus draws closer to the concerns of traditional metaphysics, even borrowing many easily identifiable notions from metaphysics, although his phenomenological method gives them a new aspect. In doing this he departs sharply from Kierkegaard, most of all when he denies that God is a necessary factor in transcendence.

IV

In a way, in departing from Kierkegaard, Heidegger draws close to Jaspers, who likewise denies that a notion of God is a necessary element in transcendence. However Jaspers by this denial does not suppress the notion but only secularizes it. He does not deny that God exists but only that his existence has no essential relation to man's discovering through aversion to the rational of the truth of being.

For Jaspers man can pursue this goal while remaining locked up within himself. He does not need, for this purpose, to reach out for God. He cannot, in fact, through this process reach out for God. In this conclusion, Jaspers, just as Heidegger, starting from an Existential nausea similar to Kierkegaard's, arrives at a totally different interpretation of being.

For Jaspers, man in arising from *ratio* to true insight into being throws off the limitations of the rational. Instead of its restrictions, he embraces the freedom of the infinite. But this free thing which he so embraces is his own being. This he knows without relating it to anything outside, in particular to a transcendent God. He therefore in his true knowledge of being has no place for God. Even if God exists, he is unattainable and therefore has no cognitive significance. Without reference to God man can quite well explain himself. This conviction, so different from Kierkegaard's, nevertheless originates in precisely the same existential nausea for the rational.

The root of this diversity of doctrinal content in spite of its common source is due, as we have already seen, to the logical fact that the source is a pure negation. It tells the mind only what the truth is not, and, therefore, leaves it undetermined as to what positively is the truth. The mind must determine truth for itself, and since it must do so basing itself on the contingent personal inclinations of the different thinkers in which it manifests itself, it thereby creates a pluralism of doctrine—a variety of doctrine which also involves antithesis. Thus, while making them all one in their irrationality, it makes them man's in their particular forms of this. Thus they mirror theism and atheism; ontologism and anti-ontologism; philosophy and anti-intellectualism; the crassest paganism and orthodox Christianity.

V

In the version of existentialism of Gabriel Marcel orthodox Christianity is markedly the case. In his use of Catholic belief to flesh out the matter of his formal notion, the Existentialism of Marcel differs from that of Heidegger or Jaspers. In this he resembles Kierkegaard, for whom Lutheran belief served a similar purpose. Marcel made his Catholic faith preeminent. As with Kierkegaard Marcel determines the indeterminate negativity of Existential nausea by the content of faith. The result is, understandably, a different conviction from those of anti-Christian Existentialists.

For one thing, Marcel makes the openness of the soul to God far from an expendable concept. Quite the contrary, this is a necessary concept grounded in the very creatureliness of the soul. As such it makes transcendence essentially an opening of the soul to God. For the soul the experience of revulsion for the rational opens up upon the being of God, not primarily upon the true or authentic being of man as for Heidegger and Jaspers. Marcel sees the soul by the experience as coming into communion with God.

The pessimistic speculations of atheistic Existentialism are obviously far removed from this. In not promising the soul a hopeless end, but a joyful one, Marcel evokes anticipation of an abundant life to come rather than despair over the end of it all, generating charity and loyalty in the soul through which it gives it something of the greatness of the life of God. Such is the general theme of Marcel's thought. The details do no more than echo it. To see how they do this in a particular case is, nevertheless, useful in order to concretize their meaning.

From the point of view of its Existential possibilities a most interesting case in point is Marcel's analysis of the technical mentality. This analysis holds the technical mind manifests in a special way the rational approach to reality. From within the limited field of its activity it conceives of the world as made up of things capable of technological manipulation. The technical mind thinks that only such things are in the world, and their essence is to be no more than capable of manipulation. For the technological mentality this is the truth of being. Anything else is fiction. When it is so simply presented this attitude seems unnecessarily shocking, but it is nevertheless a quite common one although at times only unconsciously held. It is the attitude of those many persons who so conduct their lives as to imply that in the advance of science they expect to find its most profound answers.

Under certain critical conditions Marcel is convinced the technical mentality's attitude can cause the Existential nausea, through which alone the mind can spiritually transcend its limitations. These conditions he identifies as various critical realizations that scientific techniques cannot manipulate certain human situations. These realizations bring on the nausea.

They occur most often when the soul by various techniques endeavors to overcome death and to produce happiness. It can do neither. It has no technique by which to control death nor any by which to produce happiness. The soul not yet concretely faced with either problem needs a certain push to confront this truth. Being lethargic it tends lazily to avoid the problem and rather maintain its anticipation that science will someday provide answers. But if forced to do so the soul will confront the problem and thus experience its ineffectiveness. The resultant intense dissatisfaction is valuable since it presents the soul with the opportunity truly to participate in being.

It does this by evoking a nausea reaction for "fictitious" rational being, a nausea through which it shows the soul that this is indigestible. Again, just as the body learns by nausea that it cannot consume a certain food so the mind by nausea learns that it cannot assimilate a certain total body of doctrine. The mind by this experience also learns that it has a true food and that it must eat this, not whatever else it wants to.

By this nausea which the mind experiences when it attempts to give itself totally to the technical mentality it knows that the giving is impossible. Through this the mind also knows that the refusal to give in to this technical mentality is its good, though this is not the case when, in fact, it gives only itself halfheartedly, then it is hardly sensible to the effect. In the latter case it falls prey to a creeping and lethal paralysis without ever experiencing the extreme nausea that only the critical dosage sets off. In order to avoid this situation it would be better for the mind immediately to consume the critical dosage and thereby to precipitate the needed spiritual regurgitation, and through this to strike through to the genuine truth of being.

Such is Marcel's interpretation of the Existential reaction on the level of the technical mentality. For a soul dedicated to the pursuit of technology the nausea and despair reveal to it that it has three stages in its spiritual development:

1. In the first, it begins to live.
2. In the second, it begins to rationalize its existence and manipulate it with techniques until it realizes their fundamental inadequacy for this, and thus experiences nausea for them.
3. In the third, it penetrates through the nausea to the truth of being and thereby participates in it.

In Kierkegaard and the other Existentialists these three states, in their intentional structure, are essentially the same. In their contents however, as we have seen, they are widely different. From this comes the diversity of the Existentialist doctrines. In particular, the third stage arises in this way and brings an openness to God for some; for some despair and frustration; for others hope and joy, as for Marcel the believer.

For Marcel nausea and even despair thus have revelatory value. They show the mind its own inner states in their successive development. In its first state it experiences itself as simply being projected into the world. In its second state, it then experiences itself in its relentless urge to reason. It then experiences within this effort of reason limits which reveal to it that there is an even stronger urge than reason within it which reveals itself in nausea. The nausea arises from the attempt to seize by reason alone what reason cannot alone seize upon—the truth of being and of the self. In this realization the soul achieves authentic existence. This is the theme which Marcel ceaselessly repeats.

VI

The nausea which arises in the technical mentality may serve as revelatory, but it arises even more strongly through a false philosophical mentality. This is above all true in Positivism, which tries to convince the mind to look no further than the realm of empirical science for understanding of the world and of itself. This most powerfully imprisons the mind but no less so than arrogant Rationalism that claims to deduce "the all" from abstract principles of reason—even to deduce contingency and liberty. To do this lies beyond its power since the real truth of being is irrational. One breaks through to the knowledge of this by rejecting Positivism and Rationalism except as stages on the way. By the breakthrough, one truly engages reality and the self. The thinker who experiences this is no longer an outside observer, but a participant.

In the preceding, the unity and the diversity of the thought of Kierkegaard, Heidegger, Jaspers, and Marcel is evident. While they all build it upon the same intentional substratum, they employ quite different plans. As we have seen, the reason for this is the indetermination of that substratum which is indifferent to the structure reared upon it. Leaving the specification to the individual

VARIETIES OF EXISTENTIAL DOCTRINE

thinkers who choose it by different norms indicates only the unity of the substratum. The final result is wide diversity.

By carrying on the discussion at the level to which Heidegger brought it the principle at work here can be most lucidly seen. It is the principle of Existential dialectics. It involves, first of all, the denial that being is rational, and second, the determination of this negative content. Since being as rational content is universal, an essence, and a genus, being as negated is just the opposite—a non-universal content, an isolated subjectivity. This makes being to be a non-essence since this too is not an essence which may be identified with existence. Thus the truth of being is not essential, but existential. Affirming this Heidegger makes Existentialism a new metaphysical searching for its meaning of being.

Kierkegaard, on the other hand, makes it a theology. Where others, supposing the notion of God to be rational and as such expendable, give their Existentialism an anti-theological form, Kierkegaard makes it a means of reaching God. Thus for each thinker the non-rational of Existentialism means something different according to how each one differently conceives of the rational. This is then the root of the diversity of their various Existential doctrines. The fact that non-rational being may mean irrational being or pure nothingness or individual subjectivity or the negation of essence, and so many other such things is responsible for this. Thus, as each particular thinker accepts one or the other of these, he distinguishes his Existential thought.

Before bringing this discussion to a close we must mention briefly another body of thought which, though it is not strictly a specific variant of Existentialism, nonetheless applies to it. The exegetical Existentialism of some recent thinkers, of whom we will consider only Bultmann, is an example of this.

As this contemporary Protestant thinker sees it philosophy has in theory a twofold use. It defends theology from hostile attack, and it clarifies its fundamental ontological presuppositions, thereby providing insight into its nature. In this second use it has an intrinsic relation to theology which it does not have in the first. Bultmann most perfectly realizes this relation. Bultmann feels the philosophy of Existentialism alone gives an adequate account of the ontological significance of the theological subject but realizes this second use. He therefore feels justified in bringing it to bear upon the interpretation of the biblical text. How he does this is interesting to study.

One particular such case is the notion of his Pauline exegesis of body. As a prelude to giving this exegesis he first sharply distinguishes between the notion of body in Greek metaphysics and in Existentialism. In the former, body is a substantial thing opposed by spirit. This understanding of it makes the interpretation of the Pauline notion of "spiritual body" extremely awkward if not impossible. Necessarily, such a thing as "spiritual body" must be understood as an intermediate substance between spirit and body. This interpretation is embarrassingly animistic. Moreover it negates the Pauline notion of personal immortality beyond the grave. When an Existentialist interpretation is used these difficulties disappear.

According to this interpretation, "body" is not a substance, but a way of being, specifically man's way of being in the world. In man's movement toward the possession of true being this is a passing phase. Thus, the Pauline notion of "spiritual body" becomes simply the Christian's way of being in the world—his situation in it. For Saint Paul that this is an estrangement from the truth of man's being and that it alienates man from himself, and also that this requires correction in a life to come is understandable. Thus, for Saint Paul, spiritual body or "man's being in the world" must become the spirit of "man's union with himself," not through mutating its substance but through mutating its mode of being. For Bultmann this explains Paul's conception of survival beyond the grave.

If nothing else, this doctrine is an application of a variety of Existentialism. Although much more could be said of it this much suffices for our purpose since we are interested in it only insofar as it manifests the variety of Existentialisms and thereby helps to evaluate it. This is what we shall proceed to do in the next chapter.

CHAPTER 15

AN EVALUATION OF EXISTENTIAL DOCTRINE

In evaluating Existentialism one cannot begin by doubting the genuineness of its nausea principle. All of the signs support this; besides theory lends it the strongest evidence. To deny its existence in the face of such reasonable grounds is to manifest either stubbornness or rashness. Therefore, the nature and interpretation of the phenomenon, rather than its existence, is the problem. The real problems are: what does the Existentialist nausea mean? What is its place in the growth of the spirit? What are its causes and what do they teach us?

These are the crucial questions which we have been posing and also in a general way answering. The conception of the Existentialist nausea as a sort of spiritual reaction brought on by the failure of the mind to move to its natural ultimate goal was a general answer. It appears that nature dictates the natural ultimate goal before the mind itself makes any choice and this determines the path the mind must follow. The mind may see things differently and choose to disregard this, trying arbitrarily to determine its ultimate goal, setting for itself some other ultimate goal. This is to try to establish for itself its own absolute norm of truth and goodness. When it does this it then experiences a natural revulsion which violently purges it of its contents. This restores it to its original status and thereby gives it another chance again to choose, this time with the knowledge that in choosing it is conditioned by nature. Such is the interpretation of the Existentialist nausea which we have been proposing.

To force the mind to return to its original condition nature must cause the mind to finish clearly all the factual ultimate sense of its movement, such as it had in the case of the modern scientific mind through Hegel's insight. Once it has this knowledge then nature is able to revolt. We have interpreted the nausea of Kierkegaard for the contents of the modern speculative mind as precisely this.

It is important to note, however, that this revolt is not directed so much against the steps which lead to the false goal but against the goal itself. Therefore nature rejects the steps only insofar as they are identified with the goal itself. For this reason it will allow the spirit to absorb the steps individually and for a considerable length of time and will not rise up against them until it sees that, in their congeries, they have an ultimate sense contrary to the natural one. Then and only then will it stir to life, as it did when Hegel made it clear that the ultimate sense of rational scientific progress was the perfect self-manifestation of mind. When Hegel showed this then the spirit revolted.

The diagram of the growth of the ethical life given above in chapter 8 helps one to understand exactly what happens with the rational spirit when its congeries, or indefinite series, of steps are perceived to be contrary to actually attaining the natural goal.[12] The straight horizontal line represents the directions of movement of the speculative mind from initial ignorance to final total self-knowledge. The curved lines represent its factual movement. The second line (labeled "sinful life" in the diagram) is curved to symbolize the fact that the factual movement of speculative mind has no point of contact with the final goal—it moves to this goal and yet never touches it. This is the case, for example, of that which grows continually but has no last conclusion, though finally it exhausts its object. The terminal vertical line represents perfect self-possession, which traditional philosophy holds is the natural term of rational growth. It is a state naturally possessed from the first instant of pure intellectual being, but by man only after he has passed through the intermediate states which share in something of it. The way of attaining to perfect self-possession is, for man, as in his spiritual growth.

---

[12] Ed. note. The diagram given in Chapter 8, page 45 shows progress toward the natural goal but also a path culminating at an intermediate goal. This pattern can occur in the ethical, aesthetic, and speculative spheres.

EVALUATION

As the diagram shows man in his spiritual growth moves always closer to perfect self-knowledge. With each step forward he knows himself better, and with the final step he knows himself completely. This final step is, therefore, the sense of all the preceding steps and it is one which nature chooses for him. He does not determine it himself. Through his free choice of the means nature moves him step by step toward it.

The obvious question which arises concerning this situation is: how can it allow men to move against the true goal and thereby create within himself the condition of Existential nausea? To sin is to go against the imposed end, and this is impossible. The cogent answer is that this is not in every way impossible. The diagram symbolically represents the way in which it is possible. The movement of the rational soul to its ultimate perfection, it shows, is such that it can while always approaching closer and closer to this goal, never in fact gets past a particular intermediate one. The possibility may be indicated by choosing a particular intermediate and by taking as the law of this movement that it shall by each new step advance to a point halfway between the previous position and any given intermediate goal. This law will evidently generate an indefinite series of steps all of which will move toward the ultimate goal, but none of which will get past the chosen intermediate.

Symbolically this is how man sins. A similar ethical "law" so governs the sequence of his actions that while always tending to beatitude, he factually tends to terminate his movement in some state short of it—in the possession of honor, wealth, power, or some other such thing.

Since each of the steps he thus takes is truly an intermediate one on the way to his ultimate goal his nature does not object to any one of them. For her they are good in themselves and she willingly accepts them. When she perceives that the particular law determining their sequence makes them converge at a point far short of the one she has set only then does she refuse to do this. Then, she violently resists the procedure, reversing its direction of movement and rejecting it.

This occurs in the scientific, moral, and aesthetic fields, in each of which where the spirit converges upon an intermediate goal rather than its true ultimate one. In the scientific field it converges upon the rationally beautiful. In the moral and aesthetic fields it also chooses a goal which is truly its good, but in no case its ultimate good. When nature becomes aware of this fact, she experiences revulsion because she realizes, that rather than self-possession, the alienation-from-self sense occurs.

When nature rebels in this way it teaches the mind that the terminal sense of its movement is unnatural. For example, its pursuit of the dialectical as the absolute truth of things beyond which there is no further truth is contrary to its natural absolute goal. Nature teaches the mind that dialectical science is not self-possession but something intermediate to it, and that in choosing this latter as if it were the absolute, the mind chooses alienation from self. But nature does not by this fact teach the mind that dialectical science—or any other such intermediate knowledge—is to be entirely rejected. Nature does not teach that the dialectical, in itself, is false and repugnant to it. The mistake of the great Existentialists has been, for the most part, to make this false interpretation of nature's reaction and thereby to reject the intermediate rational steps in their own proper qualities. Nature only rejects them insofar as they are ordered to an intermediate as to an ultimate. Aside from this, she sees no objection to them, but quite the contrary seeks them out as partial realization of the true ultimate of self-possession. As long as the mind so pursues them, nature will never revolt.

The mistake of the Existentialists in interpreting their experience of revulsion for the dialectical mind was to understand the revolt as covering all of the facets of this dialectic—its defining and classifying and categorizing in themselves. They thought that nature was in revolt against the rational as such. For this reason, they rejected observation and the forming of universal laws, and theorizing—all movements of rational science. They rejected the content of being which such movements imply as if nature herself had pointed out its falseness. Yet nature had not done this. She had indicated only that none of these mental operations may be looked upon as an *ultimate* goal.

The Existentialists on seeing this message misinterpreted nature's intention, where traditional doctrine could have provided the needed insight. It could have shown them the connection between the various stages of the development of rational thought—how each lower one passes into the next higher and is therefore necessary for the latter's emergence. It could have shown them the entire process terminates in full self-possession, of which every intermediate is therefore a partial realization. Dialectical science in this growth makes a special contribution. It is philosophy in potency, and the next step up—philosophy—is the closest in rational thought to pure intellectual self-possession. Traditional doctrine through its metaphysical understanding could have shown all this. Because the modern mind was too prejudiced to listen, it did not do so. Inevitably, the Existential nausea was the only way out.

The way taken could give only a generic notion of the truth, not a specific one. The Existentialists have not been unaware of this defect but the extrinsic principles, such as subjective convictions by which they have endeavored to make up for this, are on the basis of Existential nausea alone. They have nevertheless been able in this error to find a great richness of thought because, in its variety, the experience itself is extremely rich. There are infinitely many possibilities of Existential nausea.

The richness so manifested comes not only from the indefinite number of intermediates that maybe chosen for the ultimate goal, but also from the indefinite number of previous steps ordered in turn to any one of them. These previous steps may, in spite of their common term, differ vastly from thinker to thinker. Where this vast difference exists, they will, while all pointing to the same terminal truth, qualitatively differ in their very pointing.

From these two courses, then—the indefinite number of possible intermediates which may be chosen as the ultimate goal and the indefinite number of previous steps which may be taken to get to any one of them—comes the richness of variation in Existentialist thought. And this is why different authors differently determine the content of the "truth." Traditional doctrine could have shown nevertheless that they all misinterpret it. This is because they use the Existential nausea as a key to the specific ultimate human goals—the nausea is not this.

Then in their conviction that truth is irrational the Existentialists are wrong. The proper conclusion is that no intermediate good can be made the ultimate since they fall short of it and are only steps to it. Not to realize this is to embrace self-alienation and self-negation. The spirit cannot accept the intermediate for the ultimate, it has no choice in the matter—it can choose the steps which it will take to self-possession but respecting this it has no choice. Self-possession is its natural goal.

Modern speculative thought therefore erred in choosing to consider dialectical science as ultimate truth. This error was not apparent at first. In this matter modern speculative thought saw itself as a perfectly free agent capable of setting for itself any goal—the captain of its own fate. But then, through the inevitable corrections which it had to make to bring theory into line with fact it learned the truth. Kant in the doctrine of the a priori forms of sensibility and thought made the first correction. But this then immediately showed up another deficiency. How could the a priori forms unite with their matter? They could do this only if both they and their matter were reduced to one common internal source. Fichte, Schelling, and then Hegel identified this with the Ego. In Hegel's theory, this Ego was dynamic. It could sustain and *had to* sustain evolution. This was what the choice of dialectical science as absolute truth finally implied. The spirit, knowing this, experienced revulsion—such a supposition it could not accept. Making dialectical science the absolute term of the speculative process was for the traditional doctrine the error. Dialectical science could never be this.

Once it perceived this error the spirit had necessarily to reject the supposition. Dialectical science is an intermediate knowledge that by forming laws and positing theories for them it moves man closer and closer to total self-possession. In this process of inducing and theorizing it is removed from self-possession; less so as inducing, and least so as theorizing. In each of these stages, it is potentially self-possessive. As it has an inner inclination to actualize this potentiality and to find a point of continuity with, or direction to, the higher principle. Without the continuity it feels a loss. It overcomes this loss in the science of metaphysics, which as the traditional doctrine taught, integrating all other sciences—suffusing them with its own self-consciousness. Since such self-conscious science belongs to it alone in its own right, it alone is wisdom.

EVALUATION

In the first book of the Metaphysics Aristotle establishes this. There he shows how metaphysics arise from dialectical science. The theories of dialectical science lead to metaphysical questions and then to metaphysical insights. In this way the lower and the higher sciences are immediately connected and through the connection are made continuous. The higher through the point of continuity, reaches down to actualize the lower. Thus the two are inescapably bound together. The prime speculative error of the modern mind was to regard dialectical science as potential to nothing higher. This was an error which sooner or later had to provoke Existential nausea.

Starting from the general notion of Being metaphysical science descends by restriction to the specific notions of particular beings. In this it differs from dialectical science which starts from the sensible singularity of material things, and through observing their regularities, rises to their specific notions. This science therefore converges on the same terminal goal as metaphysics, although from below rather than from above. Although they differ in their contents through that identical goal the two are therefore tied together. Nevertheless, by reason of their movement to the same terminal goal even in their difference they have a common stand. Missing this truth, the moderns misinterpreted both sciences. This misinterpretation caused in the speculative phase of their movement the Existential nausea. For by it they deprived dialectical science of its only access to self-conscious knowledge.

Metaphysical science, through which alone their dialectical studies of nature could have had this access, is in its own right self-conscious. It reflects upon and thus possesses itself. With the same knowledge with which it goes out to its object it turns back upon its own processes. All other sciences go out to their object but never then turn back into themselves. When we say that metaphysics alone defends itself and explains itself, we express this same truth, that it alone is self-conscious. It is of all sciences the closest to the purity and simplicity of intellectual self-possession. Other sciences approximate to this only insofar as they touch metaphysics. Touching it they become metaphysical by participation, that is to say, they become by participation self-conscious.

The evaluation of Existentialist nausea which Thomism must make is then this: that it is a necessary consequence of the mind's embracing an intermediate goal as its ultimate one. When the mind perceives the error of this, inevitably it must revolt. This is a natural process and indicates that the particular ultimate factually chosen is not the true one determined by nature. What the specific content of the latter is the revulsion of does not indicate. From the point of view of Thomism, then, this phenomenon appears genuine and useful and it has been misused by the Existential exploiters. Too often they have erred by trying to make it specify the true goal. Forcing the nausea phenomenon in this way they have falsified it. The great variety in their doctrine indicates as much.

They differ among themselves substantially on the specific content of the true goal. These divergences have been self-defeating and false to the true significance of the Existential experience. Its true message is thus mistaken. Kierkegaard has made this mistake, but perhaps even more so the more recent thinkers who spiritually depend upon him.

It does not follow from Kierkegaard's thought that all rational content is to be rejected. Neither empirical science nor philosophy—especially metaphysical—need to be depreciated. To do either on the basis of the Existential nausea is to misinterpret its significance. It does not reject the rational but only reduces it to its proper place. For the Existential nausea the rational is the indispensable means to self-possession. It is therefore rejected only to the extent that, in fact, it impedes this. It is when this occurs that the spirit revolts. This revulsion is not itself a philosophy nor does it directly give rise to one, rather it simply purges the mind. The mind, so purged, may itself then go on to create a philosophy. For the history of modern speculation and moral practice this is the full significance of Existential nausea.

In the field of moral theory the modern mind has erred, just as in science, by taking the intermediate for the ultimate. This is not a peculiarly modern error, but one made often in the past. However, in modern times it has taken on a special color from the modern scientific mentality which tends to treat it as if it were a scientific problem. Kant and Hegel in particular made this attempt. Just as the scientist took mere probabilities as the ultimate end of speculation, in the moral field the modern mind erred by taking the mediating phenomena of custom and law as terminal. So the moralist took the conventional—the potentially but not actually virtuous—as the final moral goal. To support this supposition, Kant postulated the categorical imperative, and Hegel the dynamic Ego as its ultimate grounding. By this these two thinkers showed the modern mind the sense of its moral activity. It had to be either no self-possession at all, or possession of something of God, identified with self.

Kierkegaard's moral revulsion repudiated both. This was not in principle to repudiate the conventional or the legal as such, but only to distinguish them from the absolute. As such, the conventional and the legal are a partial realization of the absolute, and, to this extent, pleasing to the spirit. Aristotle would have agreed with this. For him, virtue is not the ultimate end. It no more than points to the supernatural as does rational philosophy.

Basically this is the mistake of Bultmann and other thinkers who apply Existentialist thought to biblical exegesis. No more than Aristotelian metaphysics will this application explain their supernatural character. With respect to this, all such philosophies have only an instrumental value, or a purgative one. They can, for example, indicate that a certain line of thought is false. This is purgative. It sets the mind back to the point of origin of its speculations there to begin again the search for the true direction. If the mind can discover this true direction, it will thereby determine the soundness of a particular philosophy. It can then, as Saint Thomas did with Aristotle, assimilate this into theology. Only by this assimilation does Existential nausea contact theology and exegesis.

For this reason we therefore do not depreciate the value of Existential nausea. Quite the contrary, since it is the sole tool by which the mind can reach the truth. It tends otherwise to listen only to what it wishes to hear. Nothing will otherwise sway it from this stubbornness, not even the best and the most profound philosophical reasons. The sole means of escape for individuals caught by intermediate goals is the Existential nausea. Only when they have experienced this, and through it the error of their ways, do they then begin to appreciate for the first time the genuine truth.

The purgative value of the Existential experience is therefore crucial. We should strive adequately to understand and thus properly to use it. In this way only can we gain access to the modern mind engrossed as it is with the dialectical mode of thought of science. The Thomist finds this access extremely difficult. He cannot easily make genuine contact with the Logical Positivist, the Kantian, or the Hegelian, or the many other numerous modern philosophical types. His own traditional thought is responsible for this. Between it and the more recent thought only with difficulty can he establish intentional continuity relating them one to the other and thereby making them mutually intelligible. But he can achieve this desired result though the purgative experience of the Existential nausea.

The traditional doctrine, insofar as it is not a passive body of truths but an active gospel, can attempt to utilize the Existentialist experience. In this way, it must necessarily overflow its boundaries and seek to penetrate into others. It cannot be indifferent to other thought but must seek to illuminate and understand it. Not by pride in the possession of truth, but by such love for it, Thomism must bring its light to bear upon the many obscurities of the modern mind. Realizing its capacity for doing this it can illuminate the modern mind because it knows the true sense of rational life and the true interconnection of all its phases. In principle it alone realizes the true effect of the Kierkegaardian revolt upon the minds of those who seek refuge in the so-called philosophies of existence.

Part II

Analytic Philosophy

CHAPTER 16

LOGICAL ATOMISM

Logical Atomism was Bertrand Russell's reaction to F. R. Bradley's Monism. This doctrine of the English Hegelian seemed to Russell unreal. It postulated that the ground of all is undifferentiated Being and that the multiplicity of particular things only subsequently arises through the introduction of relations into this relation-less unity. Russell disagreed. The plurality of beings was for him *the fundamental* fact. Whatever unity they have was the result of the subsequent addition in thought of mental relations.[13]

When the reasons for Bradley's position is understood it does not then seem so ungrounded or unreal or fantastic as Russell maintained. It had behind it a respectable philosophical tradition. Not only Hegel, from whom Bradley immediately derived it, but also many of history's most profound philosophers thought it was true.

In antiquity Parmenides held a similar doctrine arguing from the common Greek philosophical opinion that the intelligibility of being depends upon its identity or unity. Being, he argued, on this basis, identifies and does not diversify. Whatever therefore diversifies must be opposed to being. But this is nothing. Therefore, nothing diversifies being, or to say the same thing, there is only one being and all appearances of diversity is illusion.

Centuries afterward, Spinoza repeated essentially the same argument. And in the early nineteenth century, Hegel attempting to

---

[13] Ernest Gellner, *Words and Things* (London: Gollanz, 1959), 71.

correct what he thought to be the defects of the Kantian critique, came to the same conclusion. The absolute beginning for the emergence of self-consciousness of Spirit is the relation-less unity of undifferentiated being.[14] This was the position that Bradley then substantially adopted.

From the point of view of common experience it does seem strange. But from the point of view of profound intellectual penetration it seems the opposite. On this the greatest of the Greek minds agreed. This is why they commonly regarded sense experience as illusion and intellectual as truth. It took the extraordinary genius of Aristotle to find a way to justify both sense and intellect; and the understanding of the metaphysical justification requires a high level of sophistication.[15]

Bradley's position was therefore not pure fantasy. The absolute beginning of all he wrote in an article is undifferentiated "felt."[16] In this beginning there are therefore no relations—initial experience is like a visual blur.

But, as Hegel has shown, this could not be the end. Beyond undifferentiated initial experience lies the multiple phenomena of mind and reality. These differentiated experiences then lead to fully self-conscious Spirit, but they are not thereby destroyed, nor is the unity of original being thereby destroyed. The return of Spirit into itself sustains both.[17]

Bradley recognized that from the point of view of common experience this doctrine seemed bizarre. But this did not bother him.

---

[14] Georg Hegel, *Phenomenology of Mind,* Rev. 2nd ed. (London: Muirhead Library of Philosophy, 1955), 149-160.

[15] Martin Heidegger, *Sein und Zeit,* 2nd ed. Rev. (Halle, 1941), 2-3.

[16] F. R. Bradley, "Association and Thought", *Mind,* vol. 12, no. 47 (July 1887), 354–81.

[17] F. R. Bradley, *Essays on Truth and Reality* (Oxford: Clarendon Press, 1914), 159-160.

LOGICAL ATOMISM

Ryle's explanation of why it did not is also bizarre.[18] Ryle pointed out that when Bradley was an undergraduate at Oxford University his classmates were mostly students for the ministry. Their chief interest naturally was in theology. Therefore they found the idea that being is one was quite acceptable.[19] By the time Russell arrived at the university the percentage of ministerial students had dropped. The idea that being is one had found less acceptance. Russell agreeing with this new assessment called it an ontological "blancmange."[20]

Bradley summed up Russell's position as: the view that what is first given in experience cannot be a undifferentiated reality, therefore if such a content is subsequently given, some intervening mental process must mediate it.[21] The intervening process could only be that of introducing relations. The mind imposes them upon the multiple reality fundamentally given in consciousness. Bradley argued that in this way Russell could never explain the unity of experience.

Russell stating his own position and not all that differently, held that the world is ultimately a plurality of things and that its unity is in consciousness. Whatever this may be is secondary. In this world, therefore, identity is not immanent in difference, but is brought to it.[22] Russell held this is true not only of reality but of thought. The thinker is ultimately a multiplicity or series of thoughts that the causal relation connects.[23] That connection is the only unity that

---

[18] Gilbert Ryle (1900-1976) was elected to the Waynflete chair, Oxford University in 1945.

[19] W. C. Kneale *et al.*, *The Revolution in Philosophy* (New York: St. Martin's Press, 1956), Introduction.

[20] Ernest Gellner, *op. cit.*, 71. Blancmange is a traditional dessert in England that is made from milk or cream, sugar and gelatin, and usually served cold. Depending on the cook it can have a variety of flavors added.

[21] Ernest Gellner, *op. cit.*, 159-160.

[22] Bertrand Russell, *The Problems of Philosophy* (London: Williams & Norgate, 1912), 142 ff.

[23] *Ibid.*

thought has. Therefore, relation does not cause the distinction of the series but unites them.[24]

In like manner mental relation causes the supposed unity of essences. They are therefore logical constructions. The prime insight of the philosopher is the recognition that this is so. And the prime function of the philosopher is to analyze the resultant logical constructs into their distinct parts so as to show their radical plurality and thus demonstrate that their relational unity, or connection is mental.[25] In one of the most sophisticated contributions to English philosophy Bradley argued that this position was untenable since it supposed the doctrine of purely external relations—a doctrine theoretically untenable.[26]

Bosanquet carried Bradley's argument forward by pointing out that whereas Russell's thought aimed at removing the notion of the one relation-less absolute, it simply replaced this with indefinitely many more. Its absolutism was therefore, in effect, more extreme.

Whatever else these arguments do they at least clarify Russell's pluralism. It was really a positing of *many* relation-less (intrinsically, that is) absolutes at the beginning of experience, each of which was similar to Bradley's one undifferentiated absolute. When it then subsequently introduced relation this had of necessity to be external. That is to say, to be such as not to constitute or even ontologically affect the beingness of the plurality. Therefore, it had of necessity to be purely mental. This mental product had then to be the object upon which the philosopher practices his form of analysis. The analysis thus touches on logical, not ontological, constructions. They were the

---

[24] *Ibid.*

[25] Bertrand Russell, *Mysticism and Logic: And Other Essays* (New York: 1918), 155.

[26] F. R. Bradley, *Essays on Truth and Reality* (Oxford: Claredon Press, 1914), 240 and 291; F. R. Bradley, *Appearance and Reality: A Metaphysical Essay* (Oxford: Clarendon Press, 1930), 574, 577, 578.

facts, or at least the subject of the facts, that valid propositions assert.[27]

Supposing that this was the true evaluation of the situation and that discourse is simply a complexus of such facts, Russell reasoned that it could not be analyzed to infinity. That is to say, its analysis would not allow of infinite regress. If this is so it follows that there must be ultimate facts and ultimate propositions that assert them. These then become his postulated atomic facts and atomic propositions. The endeavor to discover these thus become the prime object of his philosophy which he therefore appropriately designated *Logical Atomism*.

Russell in creating his philosophy of Logical Atomism in this way, as Gellner asserts, gave it the appearance of atomic physics. Although he did not reason to the existence of his atoms, he made them, likewise to atomic physics, the point of departure for all philosophical analysis and explanation.[28] Wittgenstein put this somewhat more ontologically when he stated, that unless atomic facts and propositions exist, nothing exists.[29]

Opposition to Bradley's Monism thus led Russell and Wittgenstein to this conclusion. But this opposition was not its sole source. The reductive analyses of mathematical logic, to which Russell had made such an important contribution, led him to the same conclusion.

From the point of view of ordinary discourse this conclusion seems to have a certain plausibility. Ordinary discourse seems to be a complexity that can be broken down into simpler propositions. It is reasonable to suppose that this cannot proceed into infinity. One could therefore conclude that the term would be atomic facts and

---

[27] G. J. Warnock, *English Philosophy Since 1900* (London: Oxford University Press, 1958), 33.

[28] Ernest Gellner, op. cit., 70.

[29] Ludwig Wittgenstein, *Tractatus Logico-Philosophicus* (London: Kegan Paul,1922), 2.021.

atomic propositions.[30] But from a more critical point of view, as Russell himself admitted, this analysis has a peculiar character, which seems to argue against its plausibility. The atomic propositions and the atomic facts that they state must be so evident that it is useless to state them. And the complexities to which they lead are so paradoxical that they seem to destroy themselves by their inconsistence. That is they are so paradoxical that no one will believe them.[31]

---

[30] See Bertrand Russell, "Facts and Propositions," *The Monist* 28 (Oct 1918), 495-509.

[31] Bertrand Russell, ed. Robert Marsh, *Logic and Knowledge: Essays 1901-1950* (Russell Press Ltd., 1956), 193.

CHAPTER 17

IDEAL LANGUAGE

In spite of his hesitation about paradoxical results Russell set about the prime task of Logical Atomism—the discovery of atomic propositions. He theorized, a priori, that they must consist of a proper name (a name of a particular thing) and a simple predicate. The problem was then to determine what the particular names were and what were the simple predicates. Supposing that these could be discovered he could then reconstruct complex discourse by such connectors as: "if, then"; "either, or"; and so forth.[1]

But it soon became apparent to him that such atomic propositions would have to signify three distinct facts:

1. particular facts, either positive or negative,

2. general facts, either positive or negative,

3. particular facts reducible to neither of the preceding two.

General facts must have a general name as subject and a simple predicate. It might seem that they could be reduced to particular facts as the sum to the part. But this would imply the possibility of infinite summation that Russell consistently rejected just as he had rejected infinite division. General facts had therefore to stand on their own he admitted, and they are evidently a part of discourse. He then axiomatized this conviction by affirming that whenever a fact cannot be analyzed into a finite truth-function signficate of particular atomic propositions, it is a special atomic fact, i.e., a general atomic fact.

---

[1] Warnock, *op. cit.*, 34.

Since he could not relate it even in this way with the other two atomic facts, and could in no other way explain it, but had to admit that it too was part of discourse Russell admitted the third fact only with reluctance and expressed this by qualifying it as *peculiar*. It is a statement of the sort, "Jones believes that the world is flat."[2]

His attempt to reduce this fact to particular atomic facts and general ones led Russell to develop the interesting method of elimination. In mathematics this is used to transform complex or difficult equations into simpler and more intelligible ones. Russell developed an analogous linguistic reduction by attempting to transform given sentences into others that are equivalent in sense, but which do not contain puzzling combinations of words.

Obviously if such a transformation would permit him to reduce the sentence, "Jones believes the world is flat," to atomic or general facts, he would not have to postulate this as a distinct fact. Application of the method did not permit him to do this, but it did convince him that there are still expendable elements of ordinary discourse whose removal permits the speaker to say all that he means to say without introducing needless problems. This is equivalent to asserting that the method of elimination shows a speaker all that he has a *right* to say, and what it is he has *no right* to say. The elements that he could eliminate in this way, Russell then reasoned must have no special entity to which they correspond. He designated such elements as *descriptions*.[3]

It is obvious that the elimination of such elements, if they exist, has the positive benefit of revealing those elements that cannot be eliminated. From the Empiricist point of view they must be elements to which sensibly given entities correspond. With these observations the full program for a reductive analysis is thus laid out.[4]

The result of carrying out this program, evidently, would be the discovery of a language that contains no unnecessary elements. It

---

[2] Warnock, *op. cit.*, 35.

[3] J. O. Urmson, *Philosophical Analysis: Its Development Between the Two World Wars* (Oxford: Oxford University Press 1956), 189.

[4] *Ibid.*

would be clear, unambiguous, and in one-to-one correspondence with the irreducibly given in sense experience. One could call it, from this point of view the ideal language and thus characterize the particular program for reductive analysis as a search for an ideal language.

Wittgenstein noted that this still left "in the air" the question of the epistemological status of the proposition that *asserts* the atomic fact. This calls into question the meaning of "to assert," or "to signify." And it sets the asserting proposition over and against the asserted fact. Therefore, to complete the picture one could ask what this relationship is: i.e., why it is and how it is that the assertion points to or relates to the atomic fact. Wittgenstein came to an age-old conclusion that the relationship is one of similarity. And he specified that the similarity lies in the *structure* of the elements of the proposition and the factors of the atomic fact. If this is so, he reasoned, then that is why the analysis of the former is identical with the analysis of the latter.[5] The method of reductive analysis seemed to him by this observation to be finally and fully justified. Grammatical structure is identical with ontological structure. Expression is isomorphic with fact.

When Russell wrote his article for *The Monist* of 1919, save for this addition of Wittgenstein the identity of grammatical and ontological structure was the essence of his thought.[6] The real world was a plurality of atoms tied together by relations imposed by the mind. The realm of expression has a parallel grammatical structure expressing this. By analyzing the expression, the most immediate given to consciousness, one could discover the atomic propositions, and thus through them the atomic facts.

Thus Russell at that time saw ordinary discourse as defective. This was so for the most part, although not exclusively so, because of the "peculiar facts." Ordinary discourse—whose existence he admitted as a truth-functional complex—because it contains many expendable elements is redundant and because of the pseudo-problems to which

---

[5] Gellner, *op. cit.*, 73.

[6] Bertrand Russell, "The Philosophy of Logical Atomism," *The Monist* 28, 29 (Oct 1918, Jan, Apr, Jul 1919), 495-527, 33-63, 190-222, 345-80.

redundancy gives rise is defective. If this was so, then by the elimination of the redundancy at least a considerable portion of its defectiveness could be removed. Ordinary discourse could be made more precise. This would be a movement in the direction of the ideal language. Although, it would be only an approach to the ideal, since it would still leave the problematic status of the "peculiar facts". And this would leave the resultant language not fully a truth-functional complex. A fully perfect language, he theorized at this time, would have the form of the language of the Russell-Whitehead *Principia Mathematica*.

Wittgenstein, in essential agreement with this assumption, searched for the ideal language in the two ways that the conception suggested. He tried by the method of eliminations or descriptions, to find the irreducible elements of ordinary speech. And he tried by direct creation, along the line of the Russell-Whitehead language of the *Principia Mathematica* to make the new language *ab ovo*.

In following the first method he assumed, consistent with the principles of Logical Atomism, that traditional philosophy consists nearly entirely of statements which the method of descriptions would eliminate and therefore that it was a rich mine in which to dig for these elements. He thus conducted this portion of his investigation as an attack on such philosophy. Its statements, supposing the validity of the method of descriptions, had to be nonsense. As he put it in the *Tractatus* its problems are not so much false as nonsensical.[7] The statements have to do with subjects to which nothing factually corresponds. They say nothing valid that cannot be said just as well by their total elimination. They are logical or grammatical constructions that do not correspond to Platonic entities but simply unify particulars. Therefore to speak of them as if they said something about a real world is to speak nonsense.

Wittgenstein did not conclude that by saying this, he eliminated all supposed philosophic statements. There were, for him, other such statements that had validity. These were all those that either *critique* language or tests its conformity to grammatical usage. He held such statements make sense and are philosophical. But by the very nature

---

[7] Wittgenstein, *Tractatus Logico-Philosophicus,* 4.003.

IDEAL LANGUAGE

of their origin and function they are clearly not truth-functional statements. For Wittgenstein, in the *Tractatus Logico-Philosophicus,* the totality of statements includes the propositions of natural science.[8] Therefore, none of them is a philosophical statement.[9]

Philosophy is thus less a body of propositions than an activity.[10] It is the activity of critiquing and testing, i.e., clarifying propositions that are not themselves philosophical. By this activity philosophy performs the useful task of revealing the sole valid truth-functional derivatives from atomic propositions. The philosopher teaches this art to his pupils by showing them how to avoid making nonsense statements concerning logical constructions. They must be shown that when they do make nonsense statements, they are trying to say the unsayable. The continual critique of discourse that this method requires is tedious, and the student who uses it will not, at least at first, really believe that it teaches him philosophy. But it will teach the only philosophy that makes sense, and it is the only way to do this.[11]

Wittgenstein summed up the aim of this method in the statement, "Say nothing except what can be said." He regarded traditional metaphysics as the prime violator of this exhortation. If, through the method of elimination, all its statements concerning logical construction were removed, it would have nothing to say at all. At a later date Logical Positivism made use of this same device for the same purpose—to entirely eliminate metaphysics.

Such then, was the content of Logical Atomism as Russell first formulated it in *The Monist,* and as Wittgenstein refined and polished it in the *Tractatus Logico-Philosophicus.* All that it lacked, from its point of view was the completely truth-functional language—the ideal language. The gradual emergence of the conviction on the part of

---

[8] *Ibid.,* 6.53.

[9] *Ibid.,* 4.111.

[10] *Ibid.,* 4.112.

[11] *Ibid.,* 6.53.

those who set about the search for it, that it could not be found—and therefore did not exist—led to the movement's decline.[12]

Since Logical Atomism presupposed that the world is ultimately a congeries of radically distinct atoms it was, in part, an ontology. But insofar as it also presupposed that this irreducible plurality of ultimate entities is tied together in thought by mental relations so as to produce so-called "facts," it was also a logic or theory of knowledge. Therefore, it had a twofold character that Wittgenstein further clarified. He qualified it by adding the supposition that the grammatical structure of an expression or proposition that signifies the atomic fact resembles the logical structure of the fact itself.

In the *Tractatus Logico-Philosophicus* he attempted to deduce the logical conclusions of this added supposition. There he reasoned, an atomic proposition must represent an atomic fact precisely because it resembles it in structure—and it is this that gives an atomic proposition meaning.

It would seem natural to conclude from this that molecular propositions deriving from atomic ones would similarly take their meaning because they have the same structure as molecular facts. Wittgenstein denied that this was so because he denied *that there are molecular facts.* But, he reasoned, we can still in this case say that molecular propositions have meaning if they are correctly derived from atomic propositions by the rules that govern truth-functional composition. Therefore, the truth or meaning of such propositions is secondary and derived.[13]

Taking his point of departure then in this conviction Wittgenstein tried to determine what an ideal language would be. According to Meinong's criterion—*unum nomen, unum nominatum*—its words should have a one-to-one correspondence with the things named.[14] Therefore, they would avoid ambiguity that, at this time, Wittgenstein thought to be a language defect. The ambiguously

---

[12] Warnock, *op. cit.*, 36.

[13] Warnock, *op. cit.*, 42.

[14] Alexius Meinong (1853–1920), Austrian philosopher.

named or, in other words the *indeterminately* named he held not properly to be named at all.

In his theory of descriptions Bertrand Russell had shown that such ambiguity pervades ordinary language and therefore, that to this extent, it is over laden with meaninglessness. But the same philosopher in his logical device of elimination had shown how to remove such ambiguity and make ordinary speech less ambiguous, if not entirely unambiguous; and in this way to make ordinary speech at least more meaningful. The consequence of the thoroughgoing use of this device would, of course, be the elimination of traditional metaphysical discourse. But it would also produce the ideal language and Meinong's criterion would be met.

Wittgenstein reasoned that the resultant language would resemble mathematical calculation—its propositions would resemble equations. Therefore it would have constants and variables and, just like in mathematics, it would have a general form expressed in variables, and particular forms derived by proper substitution of constants. Like mathematical calculation it would totally lack ambiguity.

From this it would follow that atomic propositions in the ideal language would be precise images of atomic facts. Since the relation of name to thing named would be one-to-one, the grammatical structure of propositions would be identical with the logical structure of the facts that they would express.

It is important to examine exactly why Wittgenstein made so much of the relationship of similarity. He seems to have stressed it because he felt the need to supply a theory of knowledge and, perhaps unconsciously, because he accepted the theory of the ancients—that knowledge is through assimilation. But this seems to occur naturally in language only in onomatopoeia. However, if knowledge is made identical with speech then it must occur in all the rest of speech. Reasoning such as this may have motivated Wittgenstein's peculiar concern.

CHAPTER 18

LOGICAL POSITIVISM

Wittgenstein having theorized upon the nature of the ideal language in a general way then tried to determine which, if any, of the propositions could be of interest to the philosopher. He concluded that only those that could describe particular states of affairs would interest him as a philosopher. But these are also the concern of the scientist. Therefore, he had to identify philosophy with science—which would eliminate it, or he would have to show its concern was different. He did the latter by supposing that although philosophy has no propositions or statements of fact that are peculiarly its own, it has a distinct way of viewing them—the concern of the philosopher is linguistic. The philosopher tests the propositions of the scientist for their meaningfulness by the criterion of the rules of language.[1]

Wittgenstein admitted that the theoretical justification of this procedure was tantamount to metaphysics. To hold that atomic propositions are similar to atomic facts is indeed to hold a metaphysical position. But this proposition is self-contradictory within his system. It is neither an atomic proposition nor a molecular one derived from atomic propositions by permissible truth-functional combinations. From the point of view of his system it is a nonsense statement. Therefore, it was quite consistent for Wittgenstein to denominate it metaphysical—that is to say, neither true nor false but entirely lacking in meaning.[2]

But this nonsense statement is at the heart of Logical Atomism and radically renders it nonsensical. The growing conviction among the followers of the doctrine that this was so led inevitably to its decline,

---

[1] Urmson, *op. cit.*, 188.

[2] Wittgenstein, *op. cit.*, 4.003.

and finally to its demise. They could hardly hold that metaphysics is nonsense on the basis of a metaphysical proposition. Ironically, Wittgenstein's forceful arguments in the *Tractatus Logico-Philosophicus* that metaphysics is nonsense were the prime cause of this result.³

But other causes contributed as well. The search for an ideal language that seemed to arise from such promising bases soon floundered. It had been thought that such a language was actually contained in ordinary discourse and that to extricate it one had only to apply Russell's method of descriptions. This would weed out and eliminate ambiguities. But the weeding out process proved tedious and soon exhausted interest. Some had thought to avoid this difficulty by constructing the ideal language a priori from the Russell-Whitehead *Principia Mathematica*. At first Wittgenstein was convinced that this was possible, and that the ideal language had, in principle, already been discovered. However, it soon developed that one could construct many languages on the same basis, so there was no unique one-to-one correspondence between atomic propositions and atomic facts. This meant that in theory atomic facts were infinite and therefore either undetectable or nonexistent.

In addition there was the difficulty of solipsism. From within the framework of Logical Atomism it was in principle impossible to determine whether the supposed atomic facts of one thinker were the same as those of another. So it was impossible for the system to claim community of doctrine.

Finally, there remained the difficulty that the search for the theoretically existent atomic propositions proved fruitless. Russell had concluded that they must exist since the analysis of ordinary discourse, or even philosophical discourse, could not proceed into infinity. But no one could, in fact, discover the term. As more and more of the searchers after this will-o-the-wisp goal became disillusioned they began to lose confidence in the presuppositions of the search.⁴

---

³ Urmson, *op. cit.*, 99, 103.

⁴ *Ibid.*, 130 ff.

At about the time this disillusionment began to gain ascendency, a new way out of the difficulties suggested itself. This new way was the so-called Principle of Verification that then grounded Logical Positivism. Most of the impetus that Logical Positivism then began to enjoy arose from the expectations that this Principle of Verification aroused.

Before its introduction to solve the impasse in Logical Positivism, the Principle of Verification already had a long history. During the course of its previous application it underwent considerable change. All of this is adequately exposed in Ayer's *Language Truth and Logic*.[5] Although, in later editions of this popular work the author modifies the Principle of Verification to counter cogent and obvious objections, in the first edition he presents the Principle in its simplest and most representative form. In this form it states that a sentence has literal meaning if and only if the proposition that it expresses is verifiable either analytically or empirically.[6] This statement applies not only to such a sentence but also to the proposition which it expresses. Other analysts, however, qualified this statement by asserting that only the proposition expressed was true or false. The sentence that expresses it they then held to be neither, but only meaningful.

A proposition was held to be analytically verifiable if it could be shown to be true solely in virtue of the meaning of its constituent symbols. In this case the predicate of the proposition is seen immediately to be identical with the subject. Ayer concluded from this interpretation that such a proposition lacks experiential content and therefore says nothing. It is, in fact, a tautology.[7]

On the other hand, an empirically verifiable proposition he held to be true because it corresponds to an actual or possible experience. In such a proposition, the predicate is not identical with the subject but rather adds something to it. But since the addition is a relation of reason the result is a logical construct. The proposition is therefore

---

[5] A. J. Ayer, *Language Truth and Logic* (London: Victor Gollanz, 1936).

[6] *Ibid.*, 5.

[7] *Ibid.*, 16.

synthetic. And since it enables the knower to anticipate the course of his experience it is also hypothetical. As such, it is a sort of prediction.[8] Thus, the Principle of Verification, so understood excludes from legitimate discourse any proposition that is not analytically or empirically verifiable—such a proposition utters nonsense.

These considerations and this conclusion seemed at first to obviate the fundamental difficulty of Logical Atomism in its fruitless search for an ideal language. Meaning was no longer to be sought in the similarity of the grammatical structure of a proposition to the logical structure of what it signified, but rather in empirical verification. This eliminated the need to discover atomic propositions.

However, it did not eliminate solipsism. Though it was naturally a serious defect in principle this was not at first attended to. But the Principle of Verification seemed so scientifically objective as to exclude subjectivity. Taking this to be the case Ayer proceeded to apply the Principle of Verification to the critique of philosophical propositions with devastating effect.

At first in this application Ayer did not concern himself greatly with the meaningfulness of identifying anticipatory-empirical propositions, hypothetical or verifiable (they were, in fact, Kant's *synthetic a priori* propositions). Later he came to believe that those propositions that expressed contents never capable of actually being experienced had to also be called verifiable. He attributed meaning to these as well if they could be held to be relevant to what *could* be experienced—even if they could not be actually experienced in themselves. But at first, as he saw the situation, he did not need to preoccupy himself with these questions but only with explaining the significance of analytical propositions.

As was customary at that time he regarded the analytic propositions as ones that experience neither confirmed nor denied. Therefore they were propositions that the "scientific mind" tended to view as arbitrary, mystical, nonsensical, and useless—as such,

---

[8] *Ibid.,* 97.

saying nothing.⁹ Ayer denied, as Kant had before him, that they were useless elements of discourse. He thought that, although they give us no real knowledge, they call our attention to the way in which we use language to speak of the real. This shows us that we do so on the basis of certain beliefs that we do not ordinarily explicate.¹⁰ As least in principle, tautologies serve the useful purpose of bringing these beliefs to mind.

Ayer tried to show that tautologies serve a useful purpose by analyzing the nature of mathematical discourse. He noted most people are convinced that mathematics is *certain* science—not merely probable or hypothetical. Then, if this is so, the propositions of mathematics must be tautologies from the point of view of Logical Positivism since empirically verifiable propositions are never certain. But, by common consent, mathematics is a *useful* science. Therefore, tautological discourse is useful discourse.

While reasoning in this way, Ayer was quite aware that the great French mathematician, Poincaré regarded it as incredible that anyone would consider mathematical propositions to be tautologies.¹¹ As every mathematician is aware one discovers and invents new truths in mathematics. Therefore, in Kantian terminology mathematical propositions must be synthetic—not analytic. Poincaré, arguing as Kant before him had done, tried to reduce mathematical discourse, even in its fundamental principles, to synthetic induction. Ayer rejected this as a meaningless metaphysical statement or at best a tautology such that the conclusions drawn from it had to be tautological too.

But Ayer went on to argue, this does not mean that they preclude invention and discovery. Because of the limitation of our faculty of reason that cannot see in one single intuitive glance all of the consequences of a definition, we must sequentially ferret them out through logical inference. If our minds did not have this limitation,

---

⁹ *Ibid.*, 79.

¹⁰ *Ibid.*, 80.

¹¹ Henri Poincaré, was a French mathematician, theoretical physicist, engineer, and philosopher of science (1854–1912).

we would have no interest in logic. That they do, in fact, have this limitation shows in so simple a case as the tautology:

$$0.91 \times 0.79 = 0.7189.$$

We cannot intuit this, to know that it is so, we infer—calculate. The inference assures us that the proposition is, in fact, a tautology, and shows why tautology in our discourse is useful and necessary.[12] Therefore, tautologies are propositions that are *a priori* true, but are useful for *a posteriori* empirical research—for "real knowledge." They help us formulate consistent statements about our empirical discoveries and correctly infer the consequences that follow from them.

The Principle of Verification thus justifies tautologies, but its prime function is to justify empirical statements—which is to say, statements of fact. These empirical statements have two levels of certitude: first is the level of conclusive certainty based on compelling evidence, second is that of inconclusive certainty based on mere probability. By the Principle of Verification those statements of fact for which evidence is conclusive are "strongly" verified; while on the other hand statements for which the evidence is merely probable are "weakly" verified. For most statements of fact this latter level of verification is all that is available to us. Therefore, most of our empirical knowledge is no more than hypothetical, and as such essentially an aid to anticipating future experience.

For Logical Positivists the Principle of Verification, so understood, seemed to remedy the essential weakness of Logical Atomism. It seemed to them one could through the consistent use of this principle actually determine what statements are valid and what facts are admissible. When they applied this conviction to the critique of the statements that classical philosophy claimed represented the truth of reality, they produced devastating results.

Ayer reasoned, on this basis that the classical propositions of philosophy could not claim to be statements of empirical fact. By their very character they could not be experienced to be true. Therefore, they had to be tautologies or nonsense. He held that they

---

[12]Ayer, *op. cit.*, 85–86.

were in good part tautologies and that their use was an exercise in linguistic analysis.[13] Therefore, they add nothing real to scientific knowledge but merely clarify its propositions linguistically. This they do by explicating their logical relationships and by defining their symbols.[14] They do this latter, not by explicating genus and species as classical logic had done and as dictionaries of ordinary language do, but by explicating usage.[15]

By *explication of usage* Ayer meant the translation of any sentence, in which a symbol (the *definiendum*) occurs in another sentence, or sentences in which the symbol or its synonyms disappear, but which has the same meaning—or as he put it—is equivalent. An example of this sort of translation is the following: the sentence "a round square cannot exist," can be translated, "no one thing can be both round and square."[16] In Ayer's opinion, this sort of translation can be so thoroughly carried out as to render the propositions of classical philosophy meaningless—in fact non-existent. Thus, he concluded that only philosophy that analyses scientific language to ferret out the logical inferences that we cannot directly intuit has validity.

A particular conclusion from this was that classical metaphysics was meaningless because all its statements make *existence* a predicate and *explication of usage* can remove it from this position in all cases. The problem of *what being is* thus disappears from meaningful discourse!

Therefore the philosophy that results from these considerations is not factual in character, but linguistic. It does not describe either physical or mental phenomena. It only analyses scientific sentences that do this to show their logical relationships and the way in which they use symbols. Philosophy so conceived, is in brief, a department of logic.[17]

---

[13] *Ibid.*, 31.

[14] *Ibid.*, 59.

[15] *Ibid.*, 60–61.

[16] *Ibid.*, 57.

[17] *Ibid.*, 58.

Of course, Ayer was quite aware that for many philosophers this conclusion would not do, but he did not allow that to disturb him. He felt that the conviction such philosophers have of saying something important about reality is an illusion occasioned by their invalid use of language.[18] For example, when they said that relations are not particulars but universals they misused language and this gave them the impression that they were stating facts. He held they were really stating something quite different, namely that relation symbols belong by definition to the class of symbols for characters, not to the class of symbols for things.[19] Thus, Ayer reduced philosophy to semantics.

When he first wrote *Language, Truth and Logic* he meant by this title the *semantics of scientific discourse.* He did not mean by this restriction to imply that the same analysis should not apply to ordinary discourse. Quite the contrary, he thought that a more extended application would have the beneficial effect of eliminating many unwarranted metaphysical assertions, and that this particular application would not be as difficult as the scientific.[20] Later, Linguistic Analysts vehemently rejected this opinion. They did so after G. E. Moore and Ludwig Wittgenstein convinced them that ordinary discourse is clearly not a simpler phenomenon than scientific discourse.

At this earlier time then it can be seen that Ayer's judgment about what philosophical analysis should be resembled Wittgenstein's view in the *Tractatus Logico-Philosophicus*—it should aim at eliminating invalid metaphysical statements. And since these seemed to arise chiefly from scientific discourse, it should concentrate on that.

Imbued with this conviction, the adherents of the linguistic movement concentrated their attention on showing how most metaphysical statements arise from misuse of language in scientific sentences—and are nonsense. Those sensitive to the feeling of metaphysicians did not accuse them of fraud; they admitted that they

---

[18] *Ibid.*, 57–58.

[19] *Ibid.*

[20] *Ibid.*, 152–153.

were truly *trying* to make sense. This was not, as Ayer said of the poets, who he claimed were deliberately bent on speaking nonsense.[21] He thought the metaphysician was trying to make sense but was trapped by language or errors of reasoning "such as that which leads to the view that the sensible world is unreal."[22]

One might think this judgment of metaphysicians implausible since they were commonly held to be highly intelligent. But Ayer held the situation was not that simple. The trap is not easily detected so that failure is not evidence of weak-mindedness. Ayer was convinced this can be shown by critically studying the language of the philosopher when he begins to *fantasize* about Being. Like all of us, the philosopher has a nearly irresistible impulse to do this, the impulse is in the very heart of speaking—language impels us. Frequently language gives existential and attributive propositions the same grammatical form. So that, from the point of view of speaking, they have the same sound grounding. As a consequence we easily fail to distinguish them.

For example, Ayer considers sentences of the type: "martyrs exist" and "martyrs suffer." These have the same grammatical form—they both consist of nouns followed by intransitive verbs. This tempts us to associate their logical types.[23] Therefore, we treat the predicate in the first in exactly the same way as we treat the predicate in the second. Thus we make "existence" or "being" a predicate, and then subsequently, a subject about which we make what we think to be valid predications. In this way, the corpus of metaphysical propositions arises by reason of an initial grammatical error. "Exist" in the first proposition is not a predicate in the same sense as "suffer" in the second proposition. G. E. Moore's argument from elimination, which resembles Russell's theory of descriptions, establishes the same point.

But if by the translation method of Ayer and the methods of Moore and Russell metaphysical propositions can be eliminated, then it

---

[21] *Ibid.*, 45.

[22] *Ibid.*

[23] *Ibid.*, 42.

follows that they must arise by an inverse process. That is to say, they must arise from valid sentences through an invalid translation. For Ayer, it was in this way that Bradley came to form the *nonsensical* statement: The Absolute enters into itself but is itself incapable of evolution or progress. There are valid and verifiable prior statements from which the proposition arises. But Ayer claims because the process by which it arose was an invalid translation it was a senseless tautology. And all other statements similar to it, such as those that affirm the unity or plurality of the world or existence of substances, are likewise meaningless for the same reason.[24] The methods of Russell and Moore lead to the same result.[25]

A particularly interesting application of these methods is in the proof for the existence of God. It shows why a widespread consensus of contemporary philosophers is that these proofs do not demonstrate the existence of a God who has the attributes of the supreme being of non-animistic religion. The so-called proofs proceed either from asserted empirical propositions—that are, by nature always only probable and therefore conclude only to the probable—or they proceed from a priori propositions that are by nature tautologies and therefore cannot conclude to real existence.[26]

In the same way, Ayer eliminated all metaphysical propositions as nonsensical statements caused by grammatical illusion.[27] The problems of valid philosophy thus become, for him, linguistic rather than factual.[28] And a valid philosophy's concern had to be not the justification of scientific statements but their internal relations and the implications of their use of symbols.[29]

For Ayer this made it impossible to divide philosophy into schools. For if philosophy asks logical questions, then it can give them

---

[24] *Ibid.*, 36, 39, 41–42.

[25] *Ibid.*, 25.

[26] *Ibid.*, 114, 115.

[27] *Ibid.*, 35.

[28] *Ibid.*, 57-59.

[29] *Ibid.*, 25.

definitive logical answers—that is to say, it excludes division. And if it asks other than logical questions then, of course, it is nonsense.[30]

This doctrine is thus clearly an attempt to advance beyond the earlier Logical Atomism through the elimination of its most fundamental defect. The Principle of Verification apparently, at least, overcame the difficulty of detecting "atomic propositions" and "atomic facts." In this way, Logical Positivism was more consistent in its anti-metaphysical approach. It also seemed to be more objective since it used a method that seemed closely akin to that of the empirical sciences. But it had its own serious defects. Consciousness of these defects was to give rise to the more contemporary school of Linguistic Analysis.

---

[30] *Ibid.*, 133, 134.

CHAPTER 19

POST-WAR DEVELOPMENTS

Logical Positivism by a more thorough application of Russell's antimetaphysical methods advanced beyond Logical Atomism. It provided a crucially necessary, explicit criterion for meaning. And it refined linguistic analysis making it to be not merely a part of the work of the philosopher, as Russell had held in common with Moore and most of the earlier analysts, but the total work.[1] In Logical Positivism, philosophy and linguistic analysis became coextensive.

However, for many philosophers this in itself was sufficient to call the movement into question. They refused to equate philosophy with linguistics. Moreover they felt that its reliance upon symbolic logic so closely associated with mathematics was exaggerated. Many felt that its wholesale abandonment of traditional philosophy was extreme. Eric Voegelin warns against an assumption that "subordinates theoretical relevance to method and thereby perverts the meaning of science."[2]

Besides this for many its technique was tedious and boring; monotonously it applied the Principle of Verification to proposition after proposition of traditional thought. Inevitably it came up with the same conclusion—nonsense. Philosophically, this was not an exciting procedure. When the procedure was applied to value judgments it led to an unpalatable nihilism.[3]

---

[1] G. J. Warnock, *English Philosophy Since 1900* (London: Oxford University Press, 1958), 56.

[2] Eric Voegelin, *The New Science of Politics: An Introduction* (Chicago: University of Chicago Press, 1952), 2-5.

[3] Ernest Gellner, *Words and Things* (London: Gollanz, 1959), 261.

Besides all this, it had serious internal defects. Not the least of these was the incapacity to maintain for long the purity of its essential criterion—the Principle of Verification. At first it was thought to be a simple and clear criterion. It soon proved to be not this at all as was vividly shown in the substantial modifications to which Ayer subjected it in the series of his editions of *Language Truth and Logic*.[4]

As the difficulties began to emerge the doctrine itself went into decline. The physical separation of its foremost disciples with the dispersal of the Vienna Circle at the beginning of the Second World War contributed greatly to this.[5] As a consequence Logical Positivism ceased to be the *predominant* movement in the broad field of Analytical Philosophy.

There was another factor that contributed to the decline of Logical Positivism. This was the growing conviction of many philosophers that language cannot be studied adequately by the techniques of reductive analysis, and thus the turning of their thoughts in other directions.[6] The philosophy that resulted from this redirection in the post-war period seemed to have little similarity with the earlier philosophy at Oxford and Cambridge. But, in fact, it was simply a flowering of ideas scattered throughout the works of earlier periods. This can be seen clearly in the evolution of the thought of John Wisdom.[7]

Wisdom's thought pre-World War Two was essentially positivistic but its peculiar stress upon analysis of language contained hints of post-war thought. He too was convinced that philosophical problems are somehow linguistic ones and therefore there would be no need

---

[4] Ed. Note. Ayer would eventually reject this work as "full of mistakes." See: Antony Flew and Roy Varghese, *There is a God* (Harper One, 2007), pp. xiv; xviii - xxiv.

[5] Warnock, *op. cit.*, 51.

[6] J. O. Urmson, *Philosophical Analysis: Its Development between the Two World Wars* (Oxford: Oxford University Press, 1956, reprint 1960), 146 ff.

[7] John Wisdom, "Philosophical Perplexities," *Proceedings of the Aristotelian Society*, Vol 37 (1936–1937), 71–88.

for philosophy if language were adequate.[8] The view taken was that a philosophical question is really a request for a ruling upon the legitimacy of a particular use of sentences. When ordinary usage supplies no clear-cut answer then something else must fill the gap—this is precisely the function of philosophy. A philosophical statement is therefore a verbal recommendation made in response to a quest for legitimacy.[9]

In this way the crucial point became the relating of philosophical statements to ordinary linguistic usage—making ordinary usage the essential arbiter of all valid statements. Such validity was to be judged—not by verification as in empirical science—but by conformity to rules that are substantially those of ordinary discourse. This was a considerable step in the direction of what was later to be known as Linguistic Philosophy. But it was only a step!

Wisdom was still convinced that ordinary language was defective, and that philosophy was its corrective. Therefore he naturally found only those philosophical theories that reveal and correct ordinary language defects to be "illuminating." Such a philosophical theory, according to this criterion, had to draw attention to likenesses and differences that ordinary language conceals.[10] In doing this it, of necessity, creates a peculiar terminology. This was the hint of the "ideal language" notion in Wisdom's earlier thought.

But it was only a hint of that idea since Wisdom had shifted his philosophical attention from reductive analysis to the comparison of philosophical statements with non-philosophical statements—ones that ordinary language sanctions. This new occupation convinced him that philosophical statements go beyond those of ordinary language—not only revealing linguistic defects—but also by explicating implicit linguistic insights.[11] Seen from this point of view, he held ordinary language tends to confuse meaning by not making explicit important implicit distinctions that it contains. Philosophy

---

[8] Urmson, *op. cit.*, 50.

[9] *Ibid.*, 173,174.

[10] *Ibid.*, 175.

[11] *Ibid.*, 175.

reveals this situation and explicates the distinctions. By doing this it penetrates into the hidden background intelligibility of language.

In his article on philosophical perplexities Wisdom gave no hint of where this line of reasoning was leading him. Probably because he did not know. However, he was fully convinced that he was on a new path and that he would by following it out discover surprising complexities in ordinary discourse.

After the Second World War English philosophy began to concern itself with this "philosophical" approach rather than with the reductive analyses of Logical Atomism and Logical Positivism. It began to study language primarily as an instrument for communication that contains its own immanent and self-validating rules of usage.[12] No clear-cut decision in its favor caused this new notion to arise. Many *ad hoc* modifications of the proceeding analytical thought made it emerge gradually until it gained wide acceptance. Then the atomic propositional, truth-functional notion of language came to be viewed as unreal. Philosophy had then to be redefined!

When Linguistic Philosophy emerged, this "new notion" was the common conviction of English philosophers. Ludwig Wittgenstein, and John Wisdom at Cambridge, and Gilbert Ryle, Friedrich Waismann, and J. L. Austin at Oxford, were the more prominent of its exponents. In the formation of this conviction the impact of Wittgenstein was easily the most influential.[13]

The "Later" Wittgenstein, as he is sometimes characterized after his discarding or contradicting of his former influential work, the *Tractatus Logico-Philosophicus,* was at first a collaborator and disciple of Russell's Logical Atomism. In his later years, this highly individualistic thinker became Logical Atomism's severest critic. His earnest efforts to apply its principles to the analysis of language brought about this change of heart. Failure in this endeavor led him then to view it as a misguided effort to construct a "queer, non-empirical account" of discourse that concealed rather than revealed

---

[12] *Ibid.,* 161.

[13] *Ibid.,* 163.

its true essence.[14] The true essence of discourse he then came to believe is a vastly more complicated phenomenon than a mere truth-functional construct from atomic propositions.

Wittgenstein saw that the common conception that the word "language" always means one and the same thing masks the fact that it is a complicated phenomenon. What are commonly called "languages" are not examples of one common essence. Their unity is rather that of a tissue of relations.[15] Their meanings are not identical as Logical Atomism and Logical Positivism had supposed them to be.

Therefore meaning could not be determined through the reduction of compound expressions to simple ones or through simple sense verification. Wittgenstein did not deny that there are compound expressions that can be analyzed and various expressions that can be verified. But he held that these are not the totality of discourse nor ever its most significant part. The most important part of discourse is the "relationality" of usage. The relations which tie words together in actual usage are the fundamental ones and give language its *fundamental* meaning. Therefore, to understand language it is necessary to primarily study these relations.

English Philosophy in following up this suggestion altered in character. It began to judge the meaning and validity of all discourse through the investigation of the norms of ordinary discourse.[16]

Once Wittgenstein had convinced himself that this is what philosophy should do, he used his new point of view to criticize Logical Positivism and Logical Atomism. He held that both of these were efforts to impose an artificial and an a priori theory on the nature of language; they took away from ordinary discourse both its flexibility and its complexity. Nevertheless, that the defective theory should do so was understandable and excusable since it was the

---

[14] Warnock, *op. cit.*, 67.

[15] Ludwig Wittgenstein, Tr. G. E. M. Anscombe, *Philosophical Investigations* 2nd. Ed. (Oxford: Blackwell Publications, 1958), Part I, p31, no. 65.

[16] Gelliner, *op. cit.*, 77.

natural consequence of an illusion to which language itself gives rise. To this extent it was not totally arbitrary.[17]

Wittgenstein was, moreover, convinced that all so-called philosophical questions arise from the same illusion.[18] The study of this illusion, its elimination, and the consequent discovery of richness of meaning of ordinary discourse became the prime philosophical task.[19] In the question of how can language give rise to such an illusion, it was thought "hardly through its proper use." Therefore misuse must be the cause. Wittgenstein termed this misuse the "bewitchment of language."[20]

Language has as its general form the expression: *this is how things are*. Although it may not appear at first sight to be the case, in the flow of ordinary discourse this is what one is saying over and over again. One has the impression of penetrating to the nature of the object of discourse but in fact one is merely moving around the frame through which one looks at that nature.[21] It is as a consequence of this that one comes to use words in an illegitimate way—the "bewitchment of language" which causes philosophical confusion.

Therefore, valid philosophical questions are only those that attempt to escape the "bewitchment". Such a question necessarily has the form: how do I escape? This articulates the consciousness that one does not know one's way. Philosophical consciousness then is properly consciousness of one's *inability* to use words correctly. Naturally full philosophical consciousness is not only awareness of the "bewitchment of language," but also of a return to correct verbal usage by properly applying the norms of ordinary discourse.[22]

---

[17] *Ibid.*

[18] Warnock, *op. cit.*, 79.

[19] Gilbert Ryle, "The Theory of Meaning," J. H. Muirhead (ed.), *British Philosophy in the Mid-Century - A Cambridge Symposium*, 1957.

[20] Warnock, *op. cit.*, 90.

[21] Wittgenstein, *Philosophical Investigations*, Part I, p. 48, no. 114.

[22] Warnock, *op. cit.*, 88.

To the question: why should one philosophize? Wittgenstein gave this answer: "To show the fly the way out of the bottle (*der Fliege den Ausweg aus dem Fliegenglas zeigen*)."[23] Such a conception of philosophy, of course, makes it neither inventive nor creative. It leaves everything as it is. The way out of the bottle is already there. The fly simply finds it and language returns to ordinary usage.

By this postulate then philosophical discourse must avoid interfering with actual speech usage that the rules of ordinary discourse legitimize. Therefore, it must not seek, as Logical Atomism and Logical Positivism did, for an ideal language which presumes to correct the defects of ordinary discourse—confining itself to the description of actual language usage it must leave everything as it is.[24] By adopting this attitude it can observe where "knots" occur in discourse through misapplication of rules and by eliminating the misapplication eliminate the "knots." Philosophers who do not do this are like primitive men who hear civilized speech. They do not understand it, or they understand it falsely. From this they draw queer conclusions.[25]

Philosophical discourse carried on according to the new norm was obviously not one method but many; and it does not place one order in things but likewise many. It is in fact like many different therapies beneficial for different diseases.[26]

The battle against "bewitchment of language" must use many therapies. To use them is the true vocation of the philosopher.[27] Linguistic Philosophy took its immediate origin from these convictions of Wittgenstein.

Linguistic Philosophy is thus based upon the premise that one should ask first, not for the meaning of words, but for their *use*. Since it is convinced that this is multiple it therefore holds that language

---

[23] Wittgenstein, *Philosophical Investigations*, Part I, p. 103, no. 309

[24] *Ibid.*, p. 49, no. 124.

[25] *Ibid.*, p. 79, no. 194.

[26] *Ibid.*

[27] Warnock, *op. cit.*, 108.

has many different sorts of truths and many correspondingly different sorts of logic with different sorts of meanings. The total context of discourse contains them, so that while words even in isolation have some meaning, this is limited and deceptive. The total context in which they are employed alone reveals and remedies this.[28]

That this is so, is evident from the fact that people generally do not distinguish synonymous words in abstraction but do so in use. If this is so then it is legitimate to conclude that actual usage gives ultimate meaning. Therefore, the philosopher should seek to ground meaning in actual usage rather than in reduction to equivalents or in verification.[29] If he finds statements that no possible experience can verify he should not conclude that they have no meaning—but rather that they have a different meaning. Their task may not be to describe how the world is but to do something quite different.[30] The philosopher is therefore that thinker who is most critically sensitive to this situation.[31]

To put it more concretely, the philosopher is the one who is critically aware that when he uses such words as "knowledge" or "being" or "object" or "I" or "proposition" or "name," and so forth, he is not primarily concerned with their meaning but rather with their proper use in conformity with the rules of the language-game in which they occur. In this way he brings meaning back from the metaphysical to the everyday.[32]

Linguistic Philosophy is thus not so much a body of doctrine as a family of methods that clarify language relationships. It is therefore not immediately concerned with the ontological structure of reality but with the grammatical structure of language. It aims to prevent misconstructions in language and thus to expose and avoid

---

[28] Urmson, *op. cit.*, 179.

[29] *Ibid.*

[30] *Ibid.*

[31] *Ibid.*, 180.

[32] Wittgenstein, *Philosophical Investigations*, Part I, p. 48, no. 116.

absurdities.[33] As Immanuel Kant endeavors to free reason from the temptation to think the unthinkable (for it) so Linguistic Philosophy tries to free language from the temptation to say the unsayable.[34]

Gilbert Ryle's *Concept of Mind* is an example of how one follower of the doctrine attempts to do this.[35] It examines statements that purport to speak of mind and body, and in doing so give rise to classical problems in post-Cartesian philosophical discourse that speak of body as something distinct from mind. Ryle sees the body to be the subject of material passions and mind the subject of spiritual operations. These statements make it impossible to correlate the two—the essence of the classical modern problem.

Ryle begins his investigation by carefully studying a collection of assertions concerning "mind." In each case he notes they refer to the material and to bodily behavior. The implicit rules that govern them therefore make it illegitimate to separate mind from body as the "modern dilemma" does. Therefore their opposition is linguistic and due to a violation of the rules of ordinary discourse, i.e., the assertions give rise to a misuse of language. By correcting this one suppresses an illegitimate problem. The "mind-body problem" is thus shown to be the result of linguistic confusion and is eliminated by linguistic clarification.

However, there is an objection, which Wittgenstein anticipated, frequently made against this sort of procedure. Its negativity seems to demolish everything of interest to philosophy. All those issues that seemed important to classical thinkers disappear from discourse. This did not matter to Wittgenstein who viewed such issues as a "house of cards." He thought that the fact they should appear substantial, important, and therefore interesting was itself an illusion. Like all illusions, it was better that they were removed.[36]

---

[33] Urmson, *op. cit.*, 165, 166.

[34] Wittgenstein, *Philosophical Investigations*, Part I, p. 48, no. 119.

[35] Gilbert Ryle, *Concept of Mind* (London: Hutchinson's University Library, 1949).

[36] Wittgenstein, *Philosophical Investigations*, Part I, p. 48, no. 118.

This is not to say that all followers of the movement agreed with Ryle that mind is such a "house of cards"—an illusion worth eliminating. Not all would hold this to be true specifically for the problem of mind. But all employed a common methodology for attacking philosophical problems. This left some neutral with respect to traditional school arguments. Therefore, they did not *a priori* exclude metaphysical statements but only *a posteriori,* after they had checked for clarity and validity according to their specific methodology.

Warnock, approving this neutralism of the method wrote that no one has any reason in principle to resent Linguistic Analysis unless he fears intellectual clarity and low-keyed argument. Therefore, the eye of the analyst is characteristically cold. He uses his pen to deflate and is often pedantic. But this is no reason to fear or hate him.[37]

Gellner in his critical work *Words and Things* bitingly rejected this claim to philosophical neutralism. He attempted to detail what in fact the concealed commitments are. He argued that whenever proper application of the method leads to metaphysical statements Linguistic Philosophy then illegitimately excludes them by the totally extraneous Principle of Verification.

At least for some of the members of the school the criticism seems valid. One could well argue that this was so in the case of J. L. Austin at Oxford.[38] Austin's application of the method was especially lucid. Although, Warnock's characterizations—pedantic, cold, deflating—apply to him, in a lecture that he delivered in 1958, he investigated the meanings of three apparently synonymous words: "intentionally," "deliberately," and "on purpose." He pointed out that the average person would say they meant the same thing. But he observed that same person if asked to interchange them in a variety of sentences would refuse to do so. Thus, the average person would say that in abstraction that they are synonymous, but in concrete usage they are not. He then argued that actual usage is essential for the ultimate interpretation of the meaning of language. The example

---

[37] Warnock, *op. cit.,* 173.

[38] John Langshaw Austin (1911–1960) was professor of Moral Philosophy at the University of Oxford.

proves the validity of the method. He further pointed out that the average person might well say, "he drinks his soup deliberately," but he will not say, "he drinks his soup intentionally," nor will he say, "he drinks his soup on purpose." This example indicates that for the average person hidden rules govern usage and these only come into play with usage. The Linguistic Philosopher endeavors to determine what these rules are.

Etymologies can provide the philosopher with clues. Sometimes these alone suffice to show why apparently synonymous words are not interchanged. In Austin's example, "deliberately" coming from the Latin *libra* signifies a scale, and therefore what is weighed in a scale. "Purposefully," on the other hand, signifies in its Latin origin, what is placed before one. "Intentionally," also of Latin origin, signifies tending toward, and therefore action tending toward an object. These *conceptual* differences explain why in usage we do not arbitrarily interchange them.

By this sort of etymological analysis one can uncover the entire conceptual background of ordinary speech. In the case in question, the etymological analysis shows how ordinary language conceptualizes implicitly the nature of choice or the structure of action that springs from choice. A similar analysis carefully carried out on all other important words would reveal the full background of ordinary discourse.

However, the results of these analyses can be quite dissimilar. Some members of the school have used them to exclude metaphysical statements, and some to include metaphysical statements. As a matter of fact without the introduction of the Principle of Verification from without it is theoretically impossible to avoid ending up in Aristotelian philosophy. This is the case since Aristotelian philosophy remained close to common language, made much of etymologies, and thought it important that philosophy should *ground* the myth. By grounding we mean provide a rational basis for the conceptual framework within which common discourse takes place. Gellner's critique in *Words and Things* makes sense as a description of those who avoid Aristotelian philosophy.

The later developments seem likely to replace the tedious concerns of Austin. Wittgenstein, the founder of the school, was concerned with the broad aspects of language, but Austin, the follower concentrated on *minutiae*. Interest in such a preoccupation is difficult to sustain and pass along to enthusiastic students. But Austin's concern to get to the implied conceptual background of language seems to live on in the movement in its renewed concern for metaphysical discourse.[39]

The claim to neutrality of many members of the school can be justified from the point of view of the content of their philosophical thought. Some, like G. E. M. Anscombe and Peter T. Geach were committed Thomists. Others, such P. F. Strawson and J. N. Findlay, moved into the field of metaphysics without feeling that they betrayed the movement. Strawson's work in *Individuals* and Findley's work on Hegel are cases in point.

---

[39] Warnock, *op. cit.*, 147–157.

INDEX

A

Abraham 60, 61, 78, 85
Absolute Spirit 7, 15, 57, 71
Anaxagoras 24
Anscombe, G. E. M. 145, 152
Aquinas, Thomas 3, 26, 28, 36, 40, 48, 55
Aristotle 7, 24, 27, 28, 30, 31, 32, 34, 35, 44, 45, 69, 93, 94, 109, 111, 116
atomic facts 119, 122, 124, 127, 129, 130, 139
atomic propositions 119, 120, 121, 122, 124, 125, 126, 127, 129, 130, 132, 139, 145
Austin, John Langshaw 144, 150, 151, 152
Ayer, A. J. 131, 132, 133, 134, 135, 136, 137, 138, 142

B

Bacon, Francis 15, 55
Bosanquet, Bernard 118
Bradley, F. R. 115, 116, 117, 118, 119, 138
Brahe, Tycho 5
Bultmann, Rudolf 101, 102, 111

C

Comte, Auguste 9, 13

D

Dialectical science 107, 108

E

Ego 24, 25, 26, 58, 60, 66, 74, 85, 87, 108, 111
Eleatics 35, 94
empirical science 5, 9, 10, 11, 12, 14, 19, 27, 29, 31, 32, 33, 34, 36, 43, 45, 46, 53, 54, 55, 57, 59, 100, 110, 143

Empiricism   17, 19, 23
Existentialism1, 49, 79, 90, 93, 96, 97, 98, 101, 102, 103

F

Findlay, J. N.   152
Fitche, J. G.   25, 26
Fourier, Charles   12, 13

G

Galileo Galilei   5, 10, 11
Geach, Peter T.   152
Gellner, Ernest115, 117, 119, 123, 141, 150, 151
God14, 23, 24, 26, 27, 28, 33, 34, 36, 46, 51, 56, 57, 58, 60, 66, 77, 78, 80, 81, 82, 83, 84, 85, 86, 87, 95, 96, 97, 98, 100, 101, 111, 138, 142

H

Hegel, G.W.F.2, 3, 7, 15, 19, 24, 26, 27, 28, 29, 31, 34, 35, 36, 40, 43, 45, 46, 47, 55, 56, 57, 58, 59, 61, 66, 71, 74, 80, 85, 87, 95, 103, 104, 108, 110, 111, 115, 116, 152
Heidegger, Martin92, 93, 94, 95, 96, 97, 98, 100, 101, 116
Hume, David2, 6, 14, 15, 16, 17, 18, 19, 23, 29, 55

I

ideal language123, 124, 126, 127, 129, 130, 132, 143, 147
Idealism   25

J

Jaspers, Karl   96, 97, 98, 100

K

Kant, Emmanuel2, 6, 7, 8, 14, 15, 16, 17, 18, 19, 21, 22, 23, 24, 25, 28, 29, 31, 33, 35, 36, 40, 43, 44, 47, 55, 65, 66, 70, 74, 108, 110, 111, 132, 133, 149
Kepler, Johannes   5
Kierkegaard, Soren7, 26, 28, 34, 36, 37, 40, 41, 52, 53, 55, 56, 57, 58, 59, 60, 61, 62, 63, 64, 65, 66, 67, 68, 69, 70, 71, 74, 78, 79, 80, 81, 85, 86, 87, 89, 90, 91, 92, 93, 95, 96, 97, 99, 100, 101, 104, 110, 111

L

Leibniz, Gottfried   17, 18, 45

INDEX

Linguistic Philosophy 2, 143, 144, 147, 148, 150
Locke, John 2, 16, 17
Logical Atomism 115, 119, 121, 123, 124, 126, 129, 130, 132, 134, 139, 141, 144, 145, 147

M

Marcel, Gabriel 8, 97, 98, 99, 100
Meinong, Alexius 127
metaphysics 12, 13, 16, 22, 23, 24, 27, 29, 30, 31, 32, 33, 35, 36, 44, 53, 74, 92, 96, 102, 108, 109, 111, 125, 129, 130, 135, 152
molecular propositions 126
Moore, G. E. 136, 137, 138, 141
myth/history conflict 39

N

nausea existential 53, 54, 57, 59, 64, 69, 72, 74, 77, 79, 80, 83, 87, 91, 92, 95, 96, 97, 98, 99, 100, 103, 104, 105, 107, 109, 110, 111, 112
Newton, Isaac 5, 6, 10, 11, 12, 15, 16, 23
Newtonian dynamics 6, 12, 14, 16, 17, 59
Nietzsche, Friedrich 2, 3, 49
Nihilism 2, 49
Nominalism 8, 30, 52
noumenal 7, 18, 19, 24, 26, 27

O

onomatopoeia 128

P

Parmenides 115
Phenomenology 3, 27, 43, 89, 90, 95, 116
Poincaré 133
Positivism 1, 8, 9, 11, 12, 14, 15, 16, 58, 65, 100, 126, 131, 133, 139, 141, 142, 144, 145, 147
Principle of Verification 131, 132, 134, 139, 141, 142, 150, 151

R

Rationalism 17, 19, 23, 100
Renaissance 5, 11, 28, 52
Russell, Bertrand 115, 117, 118, 119, 120, 121, 122, 123, 124, 126, 127, 130, 137, 138, 141, 144

Ryle, Gilbert   117, 144, 146, 149, 150

S

Saint-Simon   13
Schelling, Friedrich von 26, 28, 29, 36, 45, 55, 108
Schopenhauer, Arthur   2
Scientism   60
self-possession 43, 44, 45, 47, 48, 49, 50, 51, 52, 54, 57, 104, 106, 107, 108, 109, 110, 111
Situation Ethics   79
skepticism   39
Social science   12
Sociology   13
solipsism   130, 132
Spinoza, Baruch   29, 44, 115
Strawson, P. F.   152

T

tautologies   133, 134, 138

V

Vienna Circle   142
Voegelin, Eric   141

W

Warnock, Geoffrey 119, 121, 122, 126, 141, 142, 145, 146, 147, 150, 152
Wisdom, John   142, 143, 144
Wittgenstein, Ludwig 119, 123, 124, 125, 126, 127, 128, 129, 130, 136, 144, 145, 146, 147, 148, 149, 151

www.ingramcontent.com/pod-product-compliance
Lightning Source LLC
Chambersburg PA
CBHW030103240426
43661CB00039B/1475/J